SIMPLE & DELICIOUS
The four-ingredient cookbook

SIMPLE & DELICIOUS
The four-ingredient cookbook

Henry McNulty

OCTOPUS BOOKS

Recipe Notes

Ovens should be preheated to the specified temperature.

All spoon measures are level.

Measurements are given in Metric, Imperial and American.
Follow one set of measurements only – they are not interchangeable.

All the dishes serve 4.

First published 1985 by
Octopus Books Limited
59 Grosvenor Street,
London W1

© 1985 Octopus Books Limited

ISBN 0 7064 2332 1

Produced by Mandarin Publishers Ltd
22a Westlands Road, Quarry Bay, Hong Kong

Printed in Hong Kong

CONTENTS

Author's note

I have not included certain intrinsic culinary and seasoning elements
in the lists of ingredients, because they are basic necessities which turn up
again and again. Thus, I take for granted that you can also have ready
butter (including clarified butter), oil, stock, salt and black pepper.
Where specific amounts of these are important, they are given in
the method. Where larger quantities are required they are stated at the
end of the ingredients column. When choosing these storecupboard
items, I favour unrefined olive oil and unsalted butter,
and I prefer fresh, homemade chicken and beef stock.

A final note about an item that I have included in the lists of ingredients:
the best vinegar for cooking is made from white wine. Sherry vinegar
is also especially delectable. I avoid all vinegars with added flavourings.

INTRODUCTION

The purpose behind this book is to make eating and entertaining stylish yet simple. The dishes in this collection are, therefore, comparatively easy to prepare. They use only four ingredients or fewer, and have only four main stages to their preparation, but still achieve a high standard of variety and flavour.

It is never easy to think of new, quick meals, and it is time-consuming to prepare elaborate dishes with numerous ingredients. Yet, at the same time, we all aim for meals that look inviting and taste delectable. With this selection of recipes, I have tried to achieve the perfect balance between ease, elegance and fine flavour. Eating should also be fun, and I hope these recipes will make it so for you.

Some dishes seemed too simple to include, even in this collection. For example: bake an onion, unpeeled and without seasoning, in a hot oven for half an hour. Then remove the skin and eat. Nothing could be more simple and yet it is quite delicious.

Despite spareness of ingredients, these recipes will stimulate your taste buds. Many are unusual, original dishes that will appeal to the adventurous cook who wants to eat and entertain well with the minimum of time spent over a hot stove. And, if one or two tempt a reluctant or inexperienced cook to go on to new heights of culinary achievement, so much the better. **Bon appétit!**

NOBLE BEGINNINGS

Starters have several roles to play. Traditionally, they should stimulate the palate, and set the taste buds tingling in delightful anticipation of the main event. But they can also be served, perhaps two or three at a time, as suppers and snacks, lunches and light meals.

Whatever the occasion, you will find something here to suit your needs, from a hearty, warming soup to eat with chunks of fresh bread to a sophisticated seafood creation to serve at a dinner party. And, of course, all made with the simplest ingredients and the minimum of fuss.

Oysters in Champagne Sauce

METRIC/IMPERIAL	AMERICAN
24 oysters	2 dozen oysters
½ bottle champagne	½ bottle champagne
2 egg yolks	2 egg yolks
6 to 8 tablespoons single cream	6 to 8 tablespoons light cream

1. Open (shuck) the oysters (or if your supplier opens them, ask him to save their liquor) and remove them from their shells. Pour the oyster liquor and the champagne into a pan, add the oysters and poach them gently for 3 to 4 minutes.
2. Scrub half the shells, then rinse and dry them. Replace each oyster in a shell and arrange the shells in a baking dish.
3. Simmer the liquid until it has reduced by about a third, then leave it to cool slightly. Whisk the eggs with the cream and add them to the liquid. Let the sauce thicken over a low heat, then season it with salt and pepper.
4. Coat the oysters with the sauce and place briefly under a medium grill (broiler) until the tops are golden.

Gravlax

METRIC/IMPERIAL	AMERICAN
500 to 625 g/1 to 1¼ lb fresh salmon, boned and split	1 to 1¼ lb fresh salmon, boned and split
125 g/4 oz sugar	½ cup sugar
1 tablespoon white peppercorns, crushed	1 tablespoon white peppercorns, crushed
2 tablespoons chopped fresh dill	2 tablespoons chopped fresh dill

1. Ask your supplier to bone and split the salmon so that it will open in its skin like a book.
2. Rub the inside of the fish well with 125 g/4 oz (⅓ cup) salt, the sugar and the crushed white peppercorns. Sprinkle dill liberally inside the fish, then close it up and scatter the remaining dill over the outside.
3. Place the fish on a platter, position a small flat plate on top and weigh it down with cans of food or similar heavy objects. Place in the refrigerator to marinate like this for 24 to 48 hours. The fish will exude a liquid which you should pour off when you remove it from the refrigerator.
4. Wipe the salmon and serve it sliced, accompanied by thin slices of buttered brown bread.

Oysters in Champagne Sauce: in Dickens' time oysters always went with poverty. Here they're accompanied by champagne!

Tapenade

METRIC/IMPERIAL	AMERICAN
250 g/8 oz black olives	½ lb ripe olives
2 garlic cloves, crushed or chopped	2 garlic cloves, crushed or chopped
50 to 75 g/2 to 3 oz anchovy fillets in oil, drained and rinsed well	2 to 3 oz anchovy fillets in oil, drained and rinsed well
2 tablespoons capers, rinsed	2 tablespoons capers, rinsed

1. Stone (pit) the olives and rinse them thoroughly.
2. Put the garlic, anchovies, capers, 3 tablespoons of olive oil and some pepper into a blender or food processor and whizz them together for a few seconds.
3. Add the olives and whizz for a few seconds more. The mixture should be well blended but retain a roughish texture.
4. Spread the tapenade on warm buttered toast and serve.

NOTE: Tapenade keeps well. Put any excess into a clean jar, pour a thin layer of olive oil onto the surface, and cover the jar tightly.

Cod Pudding

METRIC/IMPERIAL	AMERICAN
450 ml/¾ pint milk	1¾ cups milk
500 g/1 lb cod	1 lb cod
1 teaspoon cornflour	1 teaspoon cornstarch
3 eggs, beaten	3 eggs, beaten

Also have ready: 125 g/4 oz (½ cup) melted butter

In a saucepan, mix a third of the milk with an equal amount of water and add a pinch of salt. Bring the mixture to the boil, turn down the heat and plunge the fish into it immediately; simmer for 12 minutes. Remove the fish and leave to cool, then skin, bone and flake it.
2. Add a little of the remaining milk to the cornflour (cornstarch) and stir to make a creamy consistency.
3. Incorporate this with the rest of the milk, the fish, eggs, melted butter, salt and pepper.
4. Spoon the mixture into a greased medium soufflé dish and place in a preheated moderately hot oven (200°C/400°F, Gas Mark 6) for approximately 30 minutes, until the pudding is just firm at the edges. Serve the pudding immediately.

Swordfish Kebabs à la Club Mediterranée

METRIC/IMPERIAL	AMERICAN
juice of 1 lemon and 4 lemon slices	juice of 1 lemon and 4 lemon slices
750 g/1½ lb swordfish, cut into 4 cm/1½ inch cubes	1½ lb swordfish, cut into 1½ inch cubes
2 green peppers	2 green peppers
2 onions	2 onions

1. Make a marinade with four parts olive oil to one part lemon juice, and salt and pepper to taste. Steep the swordfish in this for several hours or overnight.
2. Cut the peppers and onions into 4 cm/1½ inch squares.
3. Thread eight 15 cm/6 inch skewers with pieces of swordfish, pepper, and onion until each skewer is filled.
4. Place the kebabs under a hot grill (broiler), or on a spit, for 5 to 7 minutes until the fish is cooked. Serve the kebabs garnished with the halved lemon slices.

Moules Marinières

METRIC/IMPERIAL	AMERICAN
1.5 kg/3 lb mussels	3 lb mussels
1 onion, chopped	1 onion, chopped
150 ml/¼ pint white wine	⅔ cup white wine
3 tablespoons chopped fresh parsley	3 tablespoons chopped fresh parsley

1. Carefully scrub the mussels with a wire brush to remove their beards and any sand or grit. Discard any that are cracked or open.
2. Put the mussels, onion, white wine and about two-thirds of the parsley into a pot large enough to hold them comfortably.
3. Cover the pot and cook the mussels over a low heat until they are all open and the liquid is hot.
4. Transfer the mussels to a soup tureen. Add two tablespoons of butter and the rest of the parsley to the liquid in the pot. Reheat this broth if necessary, then pour it over the mussels and serve.

Swordfish Kebabs à la Club Mediterranée:
a deliciously simple, but effective local speciality from Turkey.

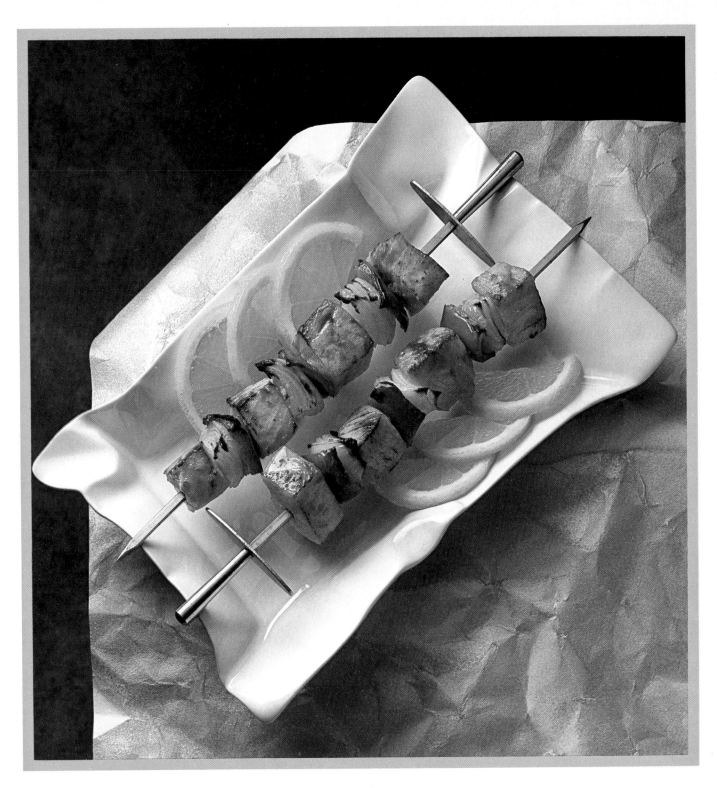

Caviar Pie

METRIC/IMPERIAL	AMERICAN
6 eggs, hard-boiled	6 eggs, hard-cooked
150 ml/¼ pint soured cream	⅔ cup sour cream
1 × 175 g/6 oz pot of black lumpfish caviar	1 × 6 oz pot of black lumpfish caviar
2 tablespoons chopped chives	2 tablespoons chopped chives

Also have ready: *125 g/4 oz (½ cup) softened butter*

1. Peel the eggs and mash them with a fork. Combine the eggs with the softened butter and add salt and pepper to taste.
2. Press the mixture into an 8 cm/3 inch deep glass baking dish, shaping it up the sides like a pie crust.
3. Mask the entire crust with a layer of soured cream and chill for 3 to 4 hours in the refrigerator (or 1 hour in the freezer).
4. Spread the caviar over the surface of the cream. (You may need to rinse the caviar first in cold water if it seems particularly salty.) Garnish the edges of the pie generously with the chopped chives. Refrigerate until ready to serve, then cut it into wedges.

Tagliolini with Smoked Salmon and Whisky

METRIC/IMPERIAL	AMERICAN
250 g/8 oz tagliolini	½ lb tagliolini
50 g/2 oz smoked salmon	2 oz smoked salmon
250 ml/8 fl oz whisky	1 cup whiskey
500 ml/18 fl oz single cream	2 cups light cream

1. Put the tagliolini into deep, boiling salted water for 8 to 10 minutes, until just tender but not soft. When it has cooked, drain it and keep it hot in the same pan.
2. While the pasta is still cooking, cut the salmon into strips. Warm the whisky in a small pan, toss in the salmon and warm through very briefly – 30 seconds only.
3. Warm the cream in another pan and add to the salmon.
4. Stir the sauce with a wooden spoon, pour onto the cooked tagliolini and serve immediately.

Leeks Provençale: the Welsh are not alone in their appreciation of leeks. This is how they are cooked in Provence.

Leeks Provençale

METRIC/IMPERIAL	AMERICAN
250 g/8 oz tomatoes	½ lb tomatoes
1 kg/2 lb leeks	2 lb leeks
about 24 black olives, stoned and chopped	about 24 pitted ripe olives, chopped
juice of 1 small lemon and 1 tablespoon of finely grated rind	juice of 1 small lemon and 1 tablespoon of finely grated rind

1. Plunge the tomatoes briefly into boiling water, then peel off the skins. Chop the tomatoes into quarters; cut a couple of quarters into slivers and set them aside for a garnish, if desired.
2. Split the leeks lengthwise and wash them, then trim and cut them into 5 cm/2 inch lengths. Simmer the leeks gently in a little olive oil for 7 minutes.
3. Add the tomatoes and olives to the leeks, turn up the heat and cook, stirring occasionally, for 3 minutes more.
4. Add the lemon juice to the mixture with salt and pepper to taste. Serve either hot or cold, garnished with the grated lemon rind and slivers of tomato, if desired.

Pumpkin Risotto

METRIC/IMPERIAL	AMERICAN
450 g/1 lb pumpkin	1 lb pumpkin
5 slices of bacon, roughly chopped	¾ cup roughly chopped bacon
150 g/5 oz long-grain rice	¾ cup long-grain rice
50 g/2 oz Parmesan cheese, grated	½ cup grated Parmesan cheese

Also have ready: *500 ml/18 fl oz (2¼ cups) chicken stock*

1. Peel the pumpkin and seed it. Cut it into 2.5 cm/1 inch cubes.
2. Heat a little olive oil in a deep casserole. Fry the bacon in this for 2 to 3 minutes.
3. Heat the chicken stock. Add the pumpkin to the bacon, and then pour in the stock and season to taste with black pepper. Cover the mixture and simmer slowly for 1 hour.
4. Add the rice to the casserole, and salt to taste. Cook the risotto, covered, for 20 minutes. Finally, stir in 1½ tablespoons of butter and the Parmesan cheese and serve.

Mushrooms Mykonos

METRIC/IMPERIAL	AMERICAN
350 g / 12 oz button mushrooms	3 cups button mushrooms
3 tablespoons vinegar	3 tablespoons vinegar
3 tablespoons tomato purée	3 tablespoons tomato paste
1½ teaspoons dried oregano	1½ teaspoons dried oregano

Also have ready: 150 ml / ¼ pint (⅔ cup) olive oil

1. Clean the mushrooms, removing the stalks if you wish.
2. Mix the olive oil with the vinegar, tomato purée (paste) and oregano in a saucepan; season with salt and pepper.
3. Bring the mixture to the boil, then simmer for 2 minutes. Add the mushrooms and cook for 10 minutes over a low heat.
4. Serve the mushrooms, either hot or cold, with the liquid spooned over.

Artichoke Hearts with Blue Cheese

METRIC/IMPERIAL	AMERICAN
8 small or 4 large, fresh artichokes	8 small or 4 large, fresh artichokes
2 tablespoons Gorgonzola or other blue cheese	2 tablespoons Gorgonzola or other blue cheese
2 tablespoons lemon juice	2 tablespoons lemon juice
3–4 tablespoons finely chopped celery	3–4 tablespoons finely chopped celery

Also have ready: 120 ml / 4 fl oz (½ cup) olive oil

1. Boil the artichokes in salted water until tender – 30 minutes to 1 hour, depending on size. When they are cooked, drain them upside down.
2. While the artichokes are still hot, remove the leaves. (Reserve them separately to eat cold later.) Cut away the 'choke' carefully, leaving the heart in a neat, dish-shaped piece.
3. Mash the cheese with a fork and add the olive oil, the lemon juice, celery, salt and a good pinch of freshly ground pepper. Taste as you mix so as not to overdo either the lemon juice or the Gorgonzola.
4. Pour onto the hot artichoke hearts and serve immediately.

Mushrooms Vigneron

METRIC/IMPERIAL	AMERICAN
500 g / 1 lb button mushrooms	4 cups button mushrooms
1 garlic clove, sliced	1 garlic clove, sliced
3 slices bacon, chopped	⅓ cup chopped bacon
120 ml / 4 fl oz red wine	½ cup red wine

1. Peel and slice the mushrooms.
2. Sauté them in a little olive oil with the garlic and bacon.
3. Cook gently for 5 minutes, then pour in the wine. Turn up the heat for 1 to 2 minutes to reduce the wine and concentrate the flavour, then continue to simmer for 2 minutes more. Add salt and pepper to taste.
4. Serve the mushrooms immediately, or allow them to cool a little and serve at room temperature.

Sliced Courgettes with Pasta

METRIC/IMPERIAL	AMERICAN
1 garlic clove, halved	1 garlic clove, halved
5 courgettes, finely sliced	5 zucchini, finely sliced
250 g / 8 oz tagliatelle	½ lb tagliatelle

1. In a large frying pan (skillet), heat a little butter (or a combination of butter and olive oil) and sauté the garlic.
2. Remove the garlic when it becomes golden brown, and gently cook the courgettes (zucchini) in the butter. Add salt and pepper to taste and continue to fry the courgettes until they are browned but not dry. Keep them hot.
3. Meanwhile, cook the tagliatelle in a deep pan of boiling water with a teaspoon of salt added, for 8 to 10 minutes or until just tender or 'al dente'. Drain the pasta and return it to the pan.
4. Tip the courgettes, with their butter, over the pasta and serve immediately. Traditionally, this dish is not served with grated cheese, but with a grind of pepper.

Sliced Courgettes with Pasta: this dish, of peasant origin, shows just how effective a simple combination can be.

Sautéed Chèvre on Radicchio

METRIC/IMPERIAL	AMERICAN
250 g/8 oz Chèvre, thick slices or small individual Crottins (see note)	½ lb goats' milk cheese, thick slices or small individual Crottins (see note)
125 g/4 oz fresh breadcrumbs	1 cup soft bread crumbs
4 large radicchio leaves	4 large red lettuce leaves
2 tablespoons walnut oil	2 tablespoons walnut oil

1. Cover the cheese with the breadcrumbs.
2. Melt a little butter in a frying pan (skillet), and fry the cheese on both sides. Use a spatula to turn them so they do not stick.
3. The cheese is done when it begins to ooze.
4. Place each portion on a radicchio leaf, sprinkle the walnut oil over the top and serve.

NOTE: Small white Chèvre cheeses, Crottins de Chavignol, can be bought in specialist food stores and easily preserved. Put the Crottins in a glass jar, cover them with olive oil and insert a few sprigs of thyme amongst them. A jar of these makes a splendid present. Remove the rind from the Crottins before use.

Omelette Arnold Bennett

METRIC/IMPERIAL	AMERICAN
6 tablespoons double cream	6 tablespoons heavy cream
25 g/1 oz smoked haddock, cooked and flaked	⅓ cup flaked, cooked smoked haddock
4 eggs, separated	4 eggs, separated
50 g/2 oz Emmental, grated	½ cup grated Emmental

1. Melt 2 tablespoons of butter with a third of the cream, add the flakes of haddock and set aside to cool.
2. Beat the egg yolks with half of the cheese, season to taste. Beat the whites and fold in; stir in the haddock.
3. Heat a knob of butter in an omelette pan. Pour in the mixture and tilt the pan so that it covers the bottom. When the omelette is cooked but still soft, slide it onto a heatproof serving dish.
4. Mix the remaining cheese and cream and spoon over the omelette. Brown it under the grill (broiler). Serve immediately.

Sautéed Chèvre on Radicchio: it's not the goat but goat's cheese that's sautéed here, and a tasty cheese it is too.

Harriet's Cheese Crisps

METRIC/IMPERIAL	AMERICAN
300 g/10 oz mature Cheddar cheese, finely grated	2½ cups finely grated sharp Cheddar cheese
250 g/8 oz plain flour	2 cups all-purpose flour
75 g/3 oz Rice Krispies	3 cups Rice Krispies
cayenne pepper	cayenne

Also have ready: 125 g/4 oz (½ cup) butter

1. Knead the cheese and the butter (both at room temperature) together with the flour and Rice Krispies, a teaspoon of salt and a pinch of cayenne pepper.
2. Pinch off small portions of dough (as much as you can hold between thumb and first two fingers).
3. Press the dough pieces flat onto lightly oiled baking sheets (you will probably need 2), leaving small gaps between each.
4. Place the baking sheets in a preheated cool oven (150°C/300°F, Gas Mark 2) for 10 minutes. To ensure even colouring, rotate the sheets after 5 minutes. When pale gold (*not* light brown), remove the biscuits (crackers) carefully with a spatula and place on a rack to cool. Keep the cheese crisps in an airtight tin to keep them fresh.

Baked Eggs with Sorrel

METRIC/IMPERIAL	AMERICAN
350 g/12 oz fresh sorrel	¾ lb fresh sorrel
grated nutmeg	grated nutmeg
4 eggs	4 eggs
120 ml/4 fl oz single cream	½ cup light cream

1. Wash the sorrel, remove the stalks and tear the leaves into strips.
2. Melt 2 tablespoons of butter in a pan over a medium heat. Add the sorrel to it and cook, stirring once or twice, for 3 to 5 minutes, until the sorrel is tender. Remove from the heat and season with a generous pinch of nutmeg, salt and pepper.
3. Divide the sorrel between four lightly buttered ramekins. Break an egg onto each bed of sorrel, cover with cream and top each with a knob of butter.
4. Put the ramekins on a baking sheet and place in a preheated hot oven (220°C/425°F, Gas Mark 7) for about 10 minutes, or until the cream begins to bubble. Remove and place the hot ramekins on individual plates to serve.

Flourless Cheese Soufflé

METRIC/IMPERIAL	AMERICAN
5 eggs, separated, plus 1 extra white	5 eggs, separated, plus 1 extra white
125 g/4 oz Ricotta cheese	½ cup Ricotta cheese
150 g/5 oz Swiss cheese (Gruyère or Emmental), finely grated	1¼ cups finely grated Swiss cheese (Gruyère or Emmental)
grated nutmeg	grated nutmeg

1. In a large bowl, combine the egg yolks with 2 tablespoons of water. Add the cheeses, a good pinch of nutmeg and salt and pepper to taste. Mix it all together until smooth.
2. Beat the egg whites until very stiff, and fold them gently into the yolk and cheese mixture.
3. Butter a soufflé dish or 4 individual ramekins and pour the mixture into it. Put the dish on a baking sheet and place in a preheated hot oven (220°C/425°F, Gas Mark 7) for 10 minutes.
4. Reduce the heat to moderately hot (200°C/400°F, Gas Mark 6) and bake for another 7 minutes for a creamy centre, or 10 minutes for a firm centre. Serve the soufflé immediately.

Fina's Classic Tortilla

METRIC/IMPERIAL	AMERICAN
750 g/1½ lb potatoes, peeled and finely sliced	4 cups finely sliced, peeled potatoes
5 eggs	5 eggs

1. Pour about 2 tablespoons of olive oil into a frying pan (skillet) (a 23 cm/9 inch pan is perfect for this amount) and cook the potatoes over low heat until tender. Remove the potatoes and drain off the oil.
2. Beat the eggs in a bowl and mix in the potatoes with some salt and pepper. Heat about 1½ teaspoons of olive oil in the frying pan and put in the egg and potato mixture. Fry gently until the underside is golden.
3. Slide the tortilla onto a plate and reverse back into the pan; fry until the new underside is also golden.
4. Slide the tortilla onto a dinner plate, place another plate on top and leave it to set and become compact. Allow it to cool to room temperature. (It is better not to refrigerate this dish.) Cut the tortilla into fudge-sized pieces and serve with an aperitif as an alternative to a first course.

Tuna and Lettuce Tortilla

METRIC/IMPERIAL	AMERICAN
6 eggs	6 eggs
1 small round lettuce	1 small round lettuce
1 × 200 g/7 oz can tuna	1 × 8 oz can tuna
juice of 1 lemon	juice of 1 lemon

1. Beat the eggs with a fork until they are frothy.
2. Wash and dry the lettuce and chop it into strips.
3. Drain off and discard the oil from the can of tuna. Flake the tuna and add it with the lettuce to the eggs, combining the ingredients thoroughly. Season the mixture with salt and pepper to taste.
4. Put 1 tablespoon olive oil into a frying pan (skillet). Pour in the tuna and egg mixture and cook over a low heat until the bottom of the tortilla has browned. Reverse the tortilla onto a plate, then slip it back into the pan and brown the other side for a few minutes. Slide the tortilla onto a serving platter and sprinkle with the lemon juice to serve.

Broccoli Custard

METRIC/IMPERIAL	AMERICAN
500 g/1 lb broccoli	1 lb broccoli
grated nutmeg	grated nutmeg
500 ml/18 fl oz single cream	2¼ cups light cream
2 eggs plus 2 egg yolks	2 eggs plus 2 egg yolks

1. Cut the broccoli stalks into chunks and cook them in boiling salted water for 5 minutes. Add the broccoli florets and cook for another 4 minutes. Refresh the broccoli under cold running water and drain.
2. Set some florets aside, then purée the rest with the stalks in a blender. Season the purée with a little nutmeg, salt and pepper. Put the purée, cream, eggs and egg yolks into a bowl and beat them together. Fold the reserved broccoli florets into the mixture.
3. Spoon the mixture into a soufflé dish and place this in a pan filled with 4 cm/1½ inches of boiling water.
4. Place the pan in a preheated moderate oven (180°C/350°F, Gas Mark 4) for 20 minutes or until a fork plunged into the custard comes out clean. Serve this dish hot or cold.

Flourless Cheese Soufflé:
believe it or not, a soufflé made without flour will rise!

Raw Celeriac Salad

METRIC/IMPERIAL	AMERICAN
500 g/1 lb celeriac root	1 lb celeriac root
1 teaspoon lemon juice	1 teaspoon lemon juice
2 tablespoons French mustard	2 tablespoons Dijon mustard
1 tablespoon wine vinegar	1 tablespoon wine vinegar

Also have ready: 120 ml/4 fl oz (½ cup) olive oil

1. Peel the celeriac and chop it into 6 cm/2½ inch chunks, then put these into a food processor and shred them. Transfer the celeriac to a bowl, pour over the lemon juice with a good pinch of salt and leave to marinate for at least 30 minutes.
2. Put the mustard into the food processor and, with the motor running, slowly add the olive oil; continue to blend until the sauce is thick and creamy. Then, still blending, gradually add the vinegar. Blend the sauce until smooth and add salt and pepper to taste.
3. Rinse the shredded celeriac in cold water and drain it.
4. Stir the mustard sauce into the celeriac. Allow the dish to rest for several hours before serving.

Pasta Shells with Green Tuna Sauce

METRIC/IMPERIAL	AMERICAN
1 × 200 g/7 oz can tuna in oil, drained	1 × 8 oz can tuna in oil, drained
3 anchovy fillets	3 anchovy fillets
40 g/1½ oz chopped parsley	1 cup chopped parsley
250 g/8 oz freshly cooked pasta shells	½ lb freshly cooked pasta shells

Also have ready: 250 ml/8 fl oz (1 cup) olive oil

1. Put the tuna and the anchovy fillets into a blender or food processor.
2. Add the parsley and some fresh ground white pepper.
3. Pour in enough of the oil to make the sauce smooth.
4. Blend the sauce for 1 minute and serve as much as desired with the freshly cooked pasta. The rest can be kept for future use.

Pasta Shells with Green Tuna Sauce:
yet another way of making pasta deliciously Italian.

Corn Chowder

METRIC/IMPERIAL	AMERICAN
1 large onion, finely sliced	1 cup finely sliced onion
4 potatoes, peeled and diced (about 350 g/12 oz)	2 cups peeled and diced potatoes (about ¾ lb)
300 g/10 oz sweetcorn kernels (preferably fresh, but frozen or canned corn will do)	2 cups whole kernel corn (preferably fresh, but frozen or canned corn will do)
1 litre/1¾ pints milk	4¼ cups milk

1. In a deep saucepan, cook the onion in plenty of butter until it is golden.
2. Add to the pan the potatoes and 500 ml/18 fl oz (2 cups) water. Cook for about 10 to 15 minutes, until the potatoes are tender.
3. Add the corn, milk, 1 teaspoon of salt and ½ teaspoon pepper. Cook the chowder for 10 more minutes without letting it boil. Adjust the seasoning at the end of cooking. (This dish improves if left to stand for a while.)
4. At serving time, heat the chowder thoroughly, pour it into four bowls and swirl a knob of butter in each one.

Courgette Soup

METRIC/IMPERIAL	AMERICAN
6 to 8 spring onions, finely chopped	6 to 8 scallions, finely chopped
500 g/1 lb courgettes, finely sliced	4 cups finely sliced zucchini
4 tablespoons soured cream	¼ cup sour cream
1 teaspoon dill weed or 2 teaspoons fresh chopped dill	1 teaspoon dill weed or 2 teaspoons fresh chopped dill

Also have ready: 750 ml/1¼ pints (3 cups) chicken stock

1. In a large saucepan, melt a little butter and sauté the spring onions (scallions) for 3 to 4 minutes.
2. Add the courgettes (zucchini) to the onions and cook, stirring, for a minute or two.
3. Pour the good chicken stock into the saucepan and simmer until the courgettes are soft. Transfer the soup to a blender or food processor and purée it; add salt and pepper to taste.
4. Serve the soup hot or cold, garnished with the soured cream and dill.

Onion Soup La Tour

METRIC/IMPERIAL	AMERICAN
500 g/1 lb Spanish onions, sliced, skins reserved	4 cups sliced Spanish onions, skins reserved
50 g/2 oz Cheddar or other hard cheese, grated	½ cup grated Cheddar or other hard cheese

Also have ready: *1 litre/1¾ pints (4¼ cups) chicken stock*

1. Melt 2 tablespoons butter in a deep saucepan and cook the onions, covered, over a low heat for about 10 minutes, until soft. Remove the lid and let the onions at the bottom of the pan brown.
2. Pour the chicken stock into a separate pan over a low heat. Wash a handful of the onion skins and add to the stock. Let them steep for 10 minutes to colour the soup, then remove them.
3. Add the stock to the onions; correct the seasoning. Warm the soup through and allow it to stand for a few minutes. Divide the cheese evenly between four bowls, pour the soup on top and serve.
4. Serve this soup with a bottle of red wine. As each person reaches his last two or three spoonfuls, pour a generous splash of wine into his bowl. This is then drunk from the bowl.

White Garlic Soup

METRIC/IMPERIAL	AMERICAN
125 g/4 oz shelled almonds	1 cup shelled almonds
2 large or 4 small garlic cloves	2 large or 4 small garlic cloves
75 to 125 g/3 to 4 oz fresh white breadcrumbs	1½ to 2 cups soft white bread crumbs
1 tablespoon vinegar	1 tablespoon vinegar

Also have ready: *120 ml/4 fl oz (½ cup) olive oil*

1. To blanch the almonds, plunge them into boiling water for a few minutes, then drain them. Their skins will slip off easily.
2. Put the almonds and garlic into a blender or food processor and whizz them well. Add the breadcrumbs and continue blending until the mixture is smooth. With the motor running, slowly add the olive oil.
3. Still blending, add 750 ml/1¼ pints (3 cups) cold water and the vinegar. The soup should have the consistency of a grainy cream; if it seems too thick, add a little more water.
4. Add salt and pepper to taste and serve the soup with an ice cube floating in each bowl.

Avgolemono with Chicken Shreds

METRIC/IMPERIAL	AMERICAN
1 small chicken breast	1 small chicken breast
4 tablespoons lemon juice	¼ cup lemon juice
2 eggs, beaten	2 eggs, beaten
1 tablespoon cornflour	1 tablespoon cornstarch

Also have ready: *1.2 litres/2 pints (5 cups) chicken stock*

1. Poach the chicken breast in the chicken stock for 5 to 6 minutes. Remove the breast and shred it.
2. In a small mixing bowl, combine the lemon juice, the eggs and the cornflour (cornstarch).
3. Ladle a spoonful of the hot stock into the egg mixture. Then pour that into the chicken stock and reheat it gently. Do not allow the soup to boil. Add salt and pepper to taste.
4. Divide the shredded chicken between four soup bowls, pour on the stock and serve.

Rosy Borstch

METRIC/IMPERIAL	AMERICAN
350 g/12 oz raw beetroot	¾ lb raw beet
2 teaspoons wine vinegar or dry sherry	2 teaspoons wine vinegar or dry sherry
120 ml/4 fl oz soured cream	½ cup sour cream

Also have ready: *600 ml/1 pint (2½ cups) beef stock*

1. Roughly slice the beetroot and boil it in 600 ml/1 pint (2½ cups) water for about 1 hour until soft.
2. Drain off the cooking liquid and reserve it. Put the beetroot briefly through a blender or food processor.
3. Simmer the beetroot purée with the cooking liquid and the beef stock for a further 15 minutes.
4. Add the vinegar or dry sherry to taste, and some salt and pepper. Divide the soup between four bowls, add a dollop of soured cream to each and mix it in well to achieve the rosy colour.

Rosy Borstch: Mother Russia has found a way of making even the lowly beetroot into a noble beginning.

–THE–
MAIN EVENT

Traditionally, the main course at a formal dinner or a family weekend feast, is the 'joint'. There are classic roasts here to satisfy the heartiest appetite with no sacrifice of flavour or elegance. However, with a little imagination and very little effort, you can also offer delicate fish dishes or more unusual meats, such as game.

Variety, after all, is the spice of life and eating one of its pleasures. So impress your family and friends with these stylish but simple main courses which will delight the palate but won't clutter up your kitchen with extraneous components.

Roast Pork with Cranberry Glaze

METRIC/IMPERIAL	AMERICAN
1.25 to 1.5 kg/2½ to 3 lb loin of pork	2½ to 3 lb loin of pork
1 kg/2 lb yams, peeled and chopped	2 lb yams, peeled and chopped
125 g/4 oz fresh or frozen cranberries	1 cup fresh or frozen cranberries
125 g/4 oz sugar	½ cup sugar

1. Sprinkle the meat with salt and pepper to taste. Place it on a rack in a roasting pan, surrounded by the yams and roast in a preheated moderate oven (180°C/350°F, Gas Mark 4); allow about 35 minutes per 500 g/1 lb of meat. Baste the pork occasionally as it roasts.
2. Test the yams with a fork to see if they are done. If they are ready before the meat, remove them and keep warm.
3. Put the cranberries into a small pan with the sugar and cook them over a medium heat for about 10 minutes or until the berries burst, forming a sauce. Ten minutes before the meat is cooked, spread it with the cranberry sauce and return it to the oven.
4. Remove the pork to a hot platter and place the yams around it.

Roast Pork with Cranberry Glaze: pork gets a fruity tang from the berries that make America's favourite breakfast drink.

Pork Casserole with Wine and Coriander

METRIC/IMPERIAL	AMERICAN
750 g/1½ lb lean pork	1½ lb lean pork
1 teaspoon flour	1 teaspoon flour
250 ml/8 fl oz dry red wine	1 cup dry red wine
2 tablespoons coriander seeds crushed	2 tablespoons coriander seeds crushed

1. Cut the pork into 2.5 cm/1 inch squares. Season the flour with salt and pepper and sprinkle it over the pork. Heat some oil in a flameproof casserole and sear the pork, turning it until all sides are evenly browned. Leave the meat over a low heat for 5 more minutes to shorten the braising time. Season the meat with salt and pepper.
2. Heat the wine in a separate pan and pour it over the pork. Stir the meat well, cover the casserole, and place it in a preheated moderate oven (160°C/325°F, Gas Mark 3) for 45 minutes. During that time you may need to add more heated wine – enough to keep the dish juicy, but not liquid.
3. After 45 minutes, add the coriander seeds and continue cooking for another 15 minutes.
4. Check that the meat is tender, stir once or twice to be sure the wine, coriander and meat are well mixed, and serve.

Cabbage with Sausage and Bacon

METRIC/IMPERIAL	AMERICAN
1 kg/2 lb white cabbage	2 lb head white cabbage
750 g/1½ lb good pork sausages	1½ lb good pork sausages
250 g/8 oz sliced bacon	½ lb bacon slices

Also have ready: *750 ml/1¼ pints (3 cups) chicken stock*

1. Cut the cabbage into eight equal wedges so that they will remain as separate portions when cooked. Blanch them by plunging them into boiling water for a few minutes.
2. Drain the cabbage portions and place them in a deep casserole.
3. Surround the cabbage with the sausages (see note below) and the bacon slices. Add the chicken stock to the casserole, and salt and pepper if desired.
4. Cover the casserole and bake in a preheated moderate oven (180°C/350°F, Gas Mark 4) for 50 minutes.

NOTE: Sausages can be even more enticingly flavoured if they are marinated. Prick them and place in 2 tablespoons olive oil with 2 tablespoons chopped onion. Marinate them for at least an hour.

Pork with Prunes and Apples

METRIC/IMPERIAL	AMERICAN
1 rack of 8 pork chops	1 rack of 8 pork chops
175 g/6 oz prunes, soaked, stoned and chopped	1 cup pitted prunes, soaked and chopped
500 g/1 lb cooking apples, peeled, cored and chopped	1 lb tart apples, peeled, cored and chopped
2 teaspoons dried thyme	2 teaspoons dried thyme

1. Ask your butcher to skin and chine the chops for easy carving, and to cut between the fourth and fifth chops so that you can bend the rack in half, backwards. Tie a piece of clean string around the rack to hold this butterfly position.
2. Mix the prunes and the apples together and add the thyme. Use this to stuff the cavity between the two sides of the rack.
3. Rub the outside of the meat with salt and pepper and place in a roasting pan with a few tablespoons of water.
4. Put the roasting pan into a preheated moderate oven (180°C/350°F, Gas Mark 4) for 1½ hours. Baste the meat occasionally and add a little more water to the pan as necessary. To serve, remove the string and carve the rack into individual chops.

Pork Sausages with Shallots and White Wine

METRIC/IMPERIAL	AMERICAN
8 shallots, peeled and chopped	2 cups finely chopped shallots
750 g to 1 kg/1½ to 2 lb good spicy pork sausages	1½ to 2 lb good spicy pork sausage links
250 ml/8 fl oz dry white wine	1 cup dry white wine
3 to 4 tablespoons finely chopped parsley	3 to 4 tablespoons finely chopped parsley

1. Melt a little butter in a flameproof dish and sauté the shallots until they are transparent but not brown.
2. Prick the sausages in several places with a skewer or a fork so that they will not burst while cooking. Place them on the bed of shallots.
3. Pour the wine over the sausages and add pepper to taste, but no salt. Place the dish in a preheated moderately hot oven (190°C/375°F, Gas Mark 5) and cook, basting frequently, for 20 to 30 minutes.
4. If there is more sauce than you like, remove the sausages and place the dish over high heat to reduce the liquid. Return the sausages to the dish and sprinkle with the chopped parsley before serving.

Pork with Prunes and Apple: in olden days pickled pork and dry biscuits were sailors' fare. But they'd have preferred this!

Pork Shoulder Braised with Cabbage

METRIC/IMPERIAL	AMERICAN
1 to 1.25 kg/2 to 2½ lb pork shoulder, boned, rolled and tied	2 to 2½ lb boneless pork butt, rolled and tied
350 ml/12 fl oz white wine	1½ cups white wine
1 kg/2 lb white cabbage, sliced and roughly chopped	2 lb white cabbage, sliced and roughly chopped
2 tablespoons crushed caraway seeds	2 tablespoons crushed caraway seeds

1. Melt some butter in a flameproof casserole and brown the pork quickly on all sides. Add salt and pepper and half of the wine. Cover the casserole and place in a preheated moderate oven (180°C/350°F, Gas Mark 4) for 1¼ to 1¾ hours, or until the meat is tender.
2. While the meat is cooking, blanch the cabbage briefly in boiling, salted water; drain it well. In a large frying pan (skillet), melt some butter and add the cabbage. Cook it over a moderate heat until it is transparent and golden.
3. Pour the rest of the wine onto the cabbage and add the caraway seeds. Test for seasoning, then cover and simmer for 30 minutes, stirring occasionally to prevent burning. Combine the cabbage with the pork and return the casserole to the oven for a final 30 minutes.
4. Transfer the cabbage to a warmed serving platter and place slices of pork on top.

Who but the Portuguese would think of combining shellfish and pork? In this case they've created a worthy dish.

Portuguese Pork with Clams

METRIC/IMPERIAL	AMERICAN
1 kg/2 lb small clams	1 quart butter clams
750 g to 1 kg/1½ to 2 lb pork, cut into 2.5 cm/ 1 inch cubes	1½ to 2 lb pork, cut into 1 inch cubes
1 onion, chopped	1 onion, chopped
4 tablespoons chopped parsley	4 tablespoons chopped parsley

1. Scrub the clam shells with a stiff brush. Rinse them thoroughly and discard any with cracked or open shells.
2. Cut the fat from the pork and melt it, with some butter, in a large frying pan (skillet). Sauté the onion in this until it is transparent. Bank the onion around the edge of the pan, leaving room for the pork.
3. Brown the chunks of pork in the onion butter, making sure they are well sealed on all sides. Add more butter to the pan if needed.
4. Mix the onion and pork together, season with salt and pepper, then add the clams and the parsley. Stir everything together, cover the pan and cook over a low heat until the clams open (discard any that do not). Let the dish rest in a warm place for 30 minutes before serving, to allow the flavours to blend.

Braised Pork with Celery Leaves

METRIC/IMPERIAL	AMERICAN
4 pork chops	4 pork chops
2 onions, chopped	2 onions, chopped
75 g/3 oz celery leaves, chopped	1 cup chopped celery leaves
120 ml/4 fl oz dry white wine	½ cup dry white wine

Also have ready: *250 ml/8 fl oz (1 cup) chicken stock*

1. Sauté the chops in a little butter until they are browned on both sides.
2. Meanwhile, melt more butter in a flameproof casserole and sauté the onions until they are translucent.
3. Place the chops in the casserole and add the celery leaves. Add the chicken stock and the wine; the liquid should barely cover the pork.
4. Put the lid on the casserole and place in a preheated moderate oven (180°C/350°F, Gas Mark 4) for 45 minutes, or until testing reveals that the chops are tender.

Silver Hearts of Veal

METRIC/IMPERIAL	AMERICAN
4 veal loin chops, 2 cm/¾ inch thick	4 veal loin chops, ¾ inch thick
75 g/3 oz ham, chopped	⅓ cup chopped ham
2 shallots, finely chopped	½ cup finely chopped shallots
500 g/1 lb mushrooms, finely chopped	4 cups finely chopped mushrooms

Also have ready: 175 g/6 oz (¾ cup) butter

1. Heat a third of the butter with 2 tablespoons oil and brown the chops quickly; add salt and pepper to taste.
2. Place each chop on a square of foil and sprinkle with ham.
3. Make duxelles by cooking the shallots in half of the remaining butter until transparent. Add the remainder of the butter and cook the mushrooms very gently for about 20 minutes. Season the duxelles with freshly ground pepper.
4. Divide the duxelles between the chops and cover each with a second piece of foil. Pinch the edges of the foil together into a heart shape and bake in a preheated moderate oven (180°C/350°F, Gas Mark 4) for 35 minutes.

Saltimbocca

METRIC/IMPERIAL	AMERICAN
8 thin slices prosciutto	8 thin slices prosciutto
8 fresh sage leaves	8 fresh sage leaves
8 thin slices of veal from the leg, pounded very flat	8 thin slices of veal from the leg, pounded very flat
120 ml/4 fl oz Italian dry white vermouth	½ cup Italian dry white vermouth

Also have ready: 500 ml/18 fl oz (2¼ cups) veal or chicken soup

1. Place a slice of ham and a sage leaf on each piece of veal. Roll the slices and fasten each with a cocktail stick (toothpick) and sprinkle with salt and pepper.
2. In a frying pan (skillet), sauté the rolls quickly in butter.
3. Add the vermouth and simmer for 2 to 3 minutes. Then add the stock and continue simmering for 25 minutes.
4. Place the rolls in a preheated moderately hot oven (190°C/375°F, Gas Mark 5) for a final 10 minutes until golden. Transfer the rolls to a serving dish and serve immediately.

Calf's Kidneys in Port

METRIC/IMPERIAL	AMERICAN
2 calf's kidneys	2 calf kidneys
1 tablespoon flour	1 tablespoon flour
120 ml/4 fl oz port wine	½ cup port wine
120 ml/4 fl oz soured cream	½ cup sour cream

Also have ready: 125 g/4 oz (½ cup) butter

1. Carefully remove skin, membrane and tubes from the kidneys. Slice them thinly and sprinkle lightly with the flour.
2. Melt the butter in a frying pan (skillet) and sauté the kidney slices quickly, stirring to ensure that they are all cooked evenly – 3 to 4 minutes should be long enough. Transfer the slices to a warm serving dish and lower the heat under the pan.
3. Add the port to the pan and stir and scrape the pan to mix the port and juices. Then stir in the soured cream over a low heat to avoid it curdling. Season the sauce with salt and pepper.
4. Pour the cream and port sauce over the kidneys and serve.

Calf's Liver à l'Orange

METRIC/IMPERIAL	AMERICAN
4 shallots, finely chopped	4 shallots, finely chopped
500 g/1 lb calf's liver, sliced	1 lb calf's liver, sliced
juice of 1 orange and the peeled, seeded segments of another	juice of 1 orange and the peeled, seeded segments of another
4 to 5 dashes of Curaçao	4 to 5 dashes of Curaçao

1. Melt 3 tablespoons butter in a frying pan (skillet) and sauté the shallots. Add the liver and cook for 2 to 3 minutes on each side.
2. Transfer the liver to a warmed serving dish, add salt and pepper to taste and keep it hot.
3. Add the orange juice to the pan, and scrape the bottom to incorporate all the meat juices. Add the orange segments and Curaçao, and heat through, then remove them from the pan and arrange around the liver.
4. Take the pan from the heat and stir 2 tablespoons of butter into the sauce; taste to see if more salt is needed. Pour the sauce over the liver and serve.

Calf's Liver à l'Orange: 'magical and mouthwatering' is the best way to describe this succulent treat.

Steak Tartar

METRIC/IMPERIAL	AMERICAN
625 g/1¼ lb very lean sirloin steak, freshly minced	1¼ lb very lean sirloin steak, freshly ground
4 eggs	4 eggs
8 anchovy fillets, finely chopped, or more to taste	8 anchovy fillets, finely chopped, or more to taste
3 tablespoons capers	3 tablespoons capers

1. In a large bowl, or on a large platter, mould the raw meat into a small, volcano-like hill.
2. Break the eggs into the hill's crater.
3. Add to the eggs the anchovy and the capers.
4. Mix together thoroughly, gradually incorporating the meat. Check the flavour for quantities of anchovies and capers, then add salt and pepper to taste. The seasoning should be quite spicy. Divide the meat into four portions to serve.

NOTE: At a dinner party, serve the four ingredients separately so that your guests can help themselves. Supply each guest with a soup plate for mixing as well as a dinner plate.

Beef Stroganoff

METRIC/IMPERIAL	AMERICAN
750 g/1½ lb best fillet steak	1½ lb best fillet steak
1 large onion, chopped	1 large onion, chopped
150 ml/¼ pint red wine	⅔ cup red wine
150 ml/¼ pint soured cream	⅔ cup sour cream

1. Trim off the fat and cut the meat into narrow little strips. In a heavy frying pan (skillet), over medium heat, melt 50 g/2 oz (¼ cup) butter in 2 tablespoons olive oil and cook the onion until it is transparent. Lift out the onions and set aside.
2. Raise the heat to high and, when the oil and butter start to smoke, add the steak and brown it evenly on all sides.
3. Lower the heat, return the onions to the pan and pour in the wine. Season the strips of meat with salt and pepper and continue cooking for a few minutes only – overcooking toughens the meat.
4. Add the soured cream, heat through gently and serve.

Entrecôte with Mustard: the English produce a large proportion of the world's mustard. Here's one tasty use for it.

Beefsteak with Capers

METRIC/IMPERIAL	AMERICAN
1 large onion, chopped	1 large onion, chopped
4 × 250 g/8 oz fillet steaks	4 × ½ lb fillet steaks
juice of 2 small lemons	juice of 2 small lemons
4 to 5 tablespoons capers	4 to 5 tablespoons capers

Also have ready: 120 ml/4 fl oz (½ cup) olive oil

1. Heat the olive oil in a frying pan (skillet) and sauté the onion. When the onion is transparent, add the steak.
2. Over a high heat, sear the steak on both sides, then reduce the heat and cook for a further 5 minutes on each side.
3. Remove the steak from the pan and keep it warm.
4. Pour the lemon juice onto the onions and, over a high heat, deglaze the pan by stirring and scraping the bottom of the pan so that the rich meat residues are amalgamated into the liquid. Add the capers to the pan and season with salt (in moderation) and pepper. Scrape the capers and juices together, pour over the steak and serve.

Entrecôte with Mustard

METRIC/IMPERIAL	AMERICAN
4 × 250 g/8 oz entrecôte steaks (4 cm/1½ inches thick)	4 × ½ lb sirloin steaks (1½ inches thick)
2 tablespoons English mustard	2 tablespoons English mustard
6 tablespoons single cream	6 tablespoons light cream
2 tablespoons cognac	2 tablespoons cognac

1. Lightly smear both sides of each steak with olive oil, then spread a little of the mustard on both sides. Pour just enough oil into a frying pan (skillet) to prevent the steaks from sticking to it, then sear the meat on both sides over a high flame. Lower the heat and cook to your taste – 3 minutes each side for very rare, 5 minutes each side for rare.
2. Set the steaks aside on a serving dish; season with salt and pepper and keep them warm, but avoid further cooking.
3. Add the rest of the mustard and half the cream to the pan and, using a fork, blend them into the pan juices; mix together well. Then, over a low heat, let the sauce reduce by about half.
4. Add the rest of the cream and the cognac to the reduced sauce, bring it just to the boil, test it for seasoning and pour it over the steaks. Serve immediately.

Entrecôte Marchand de Vin

METRIC/IMPERIAL	AMERICAN
4 × 250 g/8 oz entrecôte steaks	*4 × ½ lb sirloin steaks*
4 shallots, finely chopped	*1 cup finely chopped shallots*
500 ml/18 fl oz red wine	*2¼ cups red wine*
4 tablespoons chopped parsley	*4 tablespoons chopped parsley*

1. Melt a little butter in a heavy frying pan (skillet); salt and pepper the steaks and sauté them in the butter for about 8 minutes each side, or until cooked to your liking. Remove them from the pan and keep them warm in a serving dish.
2. Add the shallots to the pan and cook them until transparent.
3. Pour the wine (which should, by tradition, be Bordeaux) into the pan and, over a moderate heat, deglaze the pan by stirring and scraping the pan bottom to dissolve the meat residues into the wine. Then lower the heat and stir in 1 tablespoon butter.
4. Pour the sauce over the steaks and scatter the parsley over the top; serve at once.

Fillet Steak à la Moëlle

METRIC/IMPERIAL	AMERICAN
4 fillet steaks or tournedos	*4 filet mignons*
125 g/4 oz bone marrow	*¼ lb bone marrow*
3 tablespoons chopped parsley	*3 tablespoons chopped parsley*

1. Ask your butcher to give you thick, boneless steaks, cut from the heart of the fillet, and get him to lard their edges with a strip of fat. Salt and pepper both the meat and the marrow a few minutes before cooking.
2. Either quick-fry the meat in a little hot oil, or place under a hot grill (broiler) to seal. Then reduce the heat and cook the meat gently so that the lardon has time to melt a little.
3. When the steaks are done, cut the string and remove the lardon. Transfer the steaks to a serving dish; dot a small piece of butter on each and keep them hot. (Do not use the fat in which the meat was cooked.)
4. Poach the bone marrow in simmering water with some salt and pepper for 3 to 4 minutes. Remove the marrow from the bone and return to the poaching liquid until cooked. Slice the marrow and place a piece on each steak, sprinkle with the parsley and serve.

Steak au Poivre with Whisky

METRIC/IMPERIAL	AMERICAN
4 × 250 g/8 oz fillet steaks	*4 × 250 g/8 oz fillet steaks*
(4 cm/1½ inches thick)	*(1½ inches thick)*
2 tablespoons whisky	*2 tablespoons whisky*
250 ml/8 fl oz single cream	*1 cup light cream*

Also have ready: *2 tablespoons black peppercorns*

1. Crush the peppercorns by rolling a round wooden spoon handle or a rolling pin over them. Press half the pepper into one side of the steak, patting it in with your hand. Press the remaining pepper into the other side; season with salt to taste.
2. Heat a heavy frying pan (skillet) and melt 1 tablespoon butter; add the steak and sear both sides quickly. Continue cooking to your taste; 6 more minutes each side should give you a medium rare steak.
3. Transfer the steak to a hot serving dish and season with salt to taste. Add the whisky to the pan and, over low heat, mix it well with the pan juices. Pour this over the steak and serve.
4. Alternatively, if you really don't mind about calories, measure the whisky into a small ladle and ignite it with a match. Pour it over the steak while it is still in the pan. Remove the steak and keep it warm. Then add another generous splash of whisky to the pan, and stir in the cream. Blend whisky and cream with the pan juices and bring to boiling point. Spoon the sauce over the steak and serve immediately.

*Fillet Steak à la Möelle: bone marrow is often
underrated, but it is highly nutritious and full of flavour.*

Leg of Lamb en Papillôte

METRIC/IMPERIAL	AMERICAN
1.5 kg/3 lb leg of lamb	*3 lb leg of lamb*
1 to 2 garlic cloves, sliced	*1 to 2 garlic cloves, sliced*
juice of 1 lemon	*juice of 1 lemon*
1 tablespoon fresh chopped	*1 tablespoon fresh chopped*
oregano	*oregano*

1. With a sharp knife, make small slits in the lamb; insert a slice of garlic into each slit. Mix 2 tablespoons olive oil, the lemon juice, oregano, salt and pepper, and brush the entire leg with this mixture.
2. Put the meat into a roasting bag, or wrap it in greaseproof (waxed) paper. Close the bag securely, or tie the paper with string, and place the parcel on a rack in a roasting pan.
3. Put the pan in a preheated moderate oven (180°C/350°F, Gas Mark 4) and roast the meat for 15 to 18 minutes per 500 g/1 lb, for a pinkish result. (Wrapping the meat ensures that it will retain its succulent flavour and juices.)
4. Remove the roasting bag or paper, and allow the joint to rest for about 10 minutes before carving. Serve the juices as gravy.

Leg of Lamb Provençale

METRIC/IMPERIAL	AMERICAN
1.5 kg/3 lb leg of lamb	*3 lb leg of lamb*
1 small can anchovies, halved	*1 small can anchovies, halved*
2 garlic cloves, sliced	*2 garlic cloves, sliced*
1 tablespoon fresh rosemary	*1 tablespoon fresh rosemary*

1. With a sharp knife, make small slits in the meat; insert a piece of anchovy and a garlic slice into each slit.
2. Mix the rosemary with some salt and pepper and pat it over the leg.
3. Place the leg on a rack in a roasting pan and roast in a preheated moderate oven (160°C/325°F, Gas Mark 3), for 12 to 15 minutes per 500 g/1 lb for a pinkish result.
4. Remove the roast from the oven and allow it to rest for 10 minutes before carving and serving.

*Lamb Provençale: serve this excellent lamb roast
with Ratatouille (page 62) for a real Provençale treat.*

Souvlakia

METRIC/IMPERIAL	AMERICAN
juice of 1 lemon	*juice of 1 lemon*
1 teaspoon dried oregano	*1 teaspoon dried oregano*
1 kg/2 lb lamb or pork cut	*2 lb lamb or pork cut into 1*
into 2.5 cm/1 inch cubes	*inch cubes*
about 20 fresh bay leaves,	*about 20 fresh bay leaves,*
broken into large pieces	*broken into large pieces*

1. The real secret of the delectable taste of Souvlakia lies in its marination. Whisk the lemon juice and oregano with 3 tablespoons olive oil and salt and pepper. Marinate the meat in this mixture for at least 1 hour before cooking. Turn the meat occasionally to be sure that the marinade covers every bit of it.
2. Spear the meat on skewers (one 30 cm/12 inch skewer or two 15 cm/6 inch ones per person), spiking a piece of bay leaf between each piece of meat and its neighbour. Leave room at both ends of the skewers for handling.
3. Grill the meat over a very hot fire (preferably of charcoal) or on a rack under an oven grill (broiler). Turn the skewers to ensure that the meat is seared and brown outside but kept rare and juicy inside.
4. Sprinkle the souvlakia with a little more oregano and serve immediately, garnished with slices of lemon.

Rack of Lamb

METRIC/IMPERIAL	AMERICAN
1 rack of 8 lamb chops, best end of lamb, skinned and chined	1 rack of 8 lamb chops, rib end of saddle, skinned and chined
juice of 1 lemon	juice of 1 lemon
2 teaspoons crushed, fresh rosemary	2 teaspoons crushed, fresh rosemary
200 g/7 oz wild rice	1 cup wild rice

1. Cut the fat from the meat, if the butcher has not already done so. Mix 1 tablespoon olive oil with two-thirds of the lemon juice, salt and pepper and brush the meat all over with the mixture. Then press the rosemary over the whole rack.
2. Place the rack in a preheated moderate oven (180°C/350°F, Gas Mark 4) and roast for 30 minutes, basting frequently.
3. Cook the wild rice according to the packet instructions, or until tender, then drain and transfer to a warmed serving dish.
4. Work the remaining lemon juice into 50 g/2 oz (¼ cup) softened butter and form little individual pats. Separate the ribs and serve them on a bed of rice, with the lemon butter on each.

Stir-fried Lamb with Leeks

METRIC/IMPERIAL	AMERICAN
750 g/1½ lb lamb fillet, cut into thin 5 cm/2 inch strips	1½ lb lamb fillet, cut into thin 5 cm/2 inch strips
4 tablespoons soy sauce	¼ cup soy sauce
3 tablespoons sherry	3 tablespoons sherry
250 g/8 oz leeks, cut into narrow, diagonal strips	½ lb leeks, cut into narrow, diagonal strips

1. Marinate the lamb in the soy sauce and sherry for 20–30 minutes. Drain the lamb, reserving the marinade.
2. Heat 3 tablespoons of oil in a large frying pan (skillet) or wok. When the oil is hot add the lamb pieces and stir-fry for 2–3 minutes over a high flame. Transfer the pieces to a warmed plate.
3. Add the reserved marinade to the frying plan with 3 tablespoons of water and return to the heat. Stir-fry the leeks until they are barely tender.
4. Return the lamb to the frying pan, toss it with the leeks and reheat, stirring well, for one minute before serving.

Casserole of Spring Lamb

METRIC/IMPERIAL	AMERICAN
1.5 kg/3 lb middle neck of spring lamb (8 ribs)	3 lb spring lamb neck slices (8 slices)
120 ml/4 fl oz white wine	½ cup white wine
4 or 5 spring onions, green part included, chopped	4 or 5 scallions, green part included, chopped
1 celery stick, finely chopped	1 stalk celery, finely chopped

1. Ask the butcher to chop the lamb into 5 cm/2 inch chunks and remove about half the fat. This can be done at home, but the butcher can accomplish the task far faster! Heat a little oil in a large casserole and brown the lamb pieces on all sides.
2. Salt and pepper the meat to taste and pour in the wine. Put the casserole in a preheated moderately hot oven (200°C/400°F, Gas Mark 6) for 20 minutes, turning the pieces from time to time.
3. Melt 50 g/2 oz (¼ cup) butter in a small frying pan (skillet) and heat through the onions and the celery, without browning them.
4. About 5 minutes before the lamb is cooked, add the onions and celery to the casserole. Stir and allow 5 more minutes in the oven for the flavours to amalgamate fully, then serve.

Casserole of Spring Lamb: the French influence can be detected here in the liberal use of garlic.

Sea Bass with Olives

METRIC/IMPERIAL	AMERICAN
1 kg/2 lb sea bass, skinned and filleted	*2 lb sea bass, skinned and filleted*
1 kg/2 lb tomatoes, skinned and sieved	*4 cups peeled and strained tomatoes*
12 black olives, stoned	*12 pitted ripe olives*
1 tablespoon chopped fresh thyme	*1 tablespoon chopped fresh thyme*

1. Place the bass fillets close together in an oiled baking dish.
2. Mix 2 tablespoons olive oil with the tomatoes, olives and thyme and spoon this over the fish.
3. Place the fish in a preheated moderate oven (180°C/350°F, Gas Mark 4) and bake for 15 to 20 minutes, depending on the thickness of the fillets.
4. Season the bass with salt and pepper to taste, and serve.

Whiting in Sharp Mustard Sauce

METRIC/IMPERIAL	AMERICAN
1 kg/2 lb whiting fillets	*2 lb whiting fillets*
4 tablespoons single cream	*¼ cup light cream*
1 tablespoon chopped sour pickles	*1 tablespoon chopped sour pickles*
2 tablespoons French mustard	*2 tablespoons Dijon mustard*

1. Place the whiting fillets in a buttered baking dish and put this in a preheated moderately hot oven (200°C/400°F, Gas Mark 6) for 15 minutes.
2. The heat may cause some of the fish juices to exude; if so, pour this liquid away.
3. Mix the cream, pickles and mustard, salt and pepper together and spread this mixture over the cooked fish.
4. Return the baking dish to the oven for another 10 minutes, or until the fish is done. Serve immediately.

Sole in Wine and Vermouth

METRIC/IMPERIAL	AMERICAN
4 fillets of sole (about 1 kg/ 2 lb) with the heads and bones	*4 fillets of sole (about 2 lb) with the heads and bones*
1 tablespoon finely chopped shallots	*1 tablespoon finely chopped shallots*
120 ml/4 fl oz dry vermouth	*½ cup dry vermouth*
120 ml/4 fl oz dry white wine	*½ cup dry white wine*

1. Use the fish heads and bones to make a stock; you will need about 250 ml/8 fl oz (1 cup).
2. Sprinkle the shallots over the bottom of a buttered flameproof baking dish, large enough to hold the fillets. Arrange the fillets on top of the shallots and season them lightly with salt and pepper. Pour the fish stock, vermouth and wine over the fish.
3. Put the baking dish over a low heat and simmer for a minute. Cover the dish and place it in a preheated moderate oven (180°C/ 350°F, Gas Mark 4) for 10 minutes, or until the fish is cooked. Remove the dish from the oven and pour off the liquid into a small saucepan. Cover the fish again and return to the (turned off) oven to keep warm.
4. Boil the liquid rapidly over a high heat until it has reduced by about half. Gradually whisk in about 2 to 3 tablespoons softened butter – enough to make the sauce creamy – and check the seasoning. Transfer the fillets to a serving dish, pour over the sauce and serve.

Sole in Wine and Vermouth: a delicate little fish, sole has a mild and subtle flavour and is easy to cook.

Red Mullet with Fennel

METRIC/IMPERIAL	AMERICAN
1 kg/2 lb red mullet or sea bream	*2 lb red mullet or sea bream*
25 g/1 oz fresh fennel or 1 teaspoon dried	*1 oz fresh fennel or 1 teaspoon dried*
juice of 1 lemon and 1 lemon, sliced	*juice of 1 lemon and 1 lemon, sliced*
2 tablespoons pastis or ouzo	*2 tablespoons pastis or ouzo*

1. Mix about 4 tablespoons olive oil with some salt and pepper and brush the insides of the fish with it. Insert a sprig of fennel into each fish and brush the outsides of the fish with a little more oil.
2. Make a bed of fennel branches in an oiled baking pan and lay the fish on it. Place a slice of lemon on top of each fish.
3. Bake the fish in a preheated moderate oven (180°C/350°F, Gas Mark 4) for 30 minutes (or less if the fish are small). There is no need to turn them. When they are cooked, pour over the pastis and ignite it. Take care as pastis flames fiercely.
4. In a double boiler heat a little fennel (a branch or a few seeds) with 2 tablespoons olive oil and the lemon juice. Add the pan juices to this sauce. Garnish the fish with the remaining lemon slices and serve the sauce separately.

Baked Red Mullet with Citrus Fruit

METRIC/IMPERIAL	AMERICAN
3 large bay leaves	*3 large bay leaves*
4 × 350 g/12 oz red mullet	*4 × ¾ lb red mullet*
2 oranges	*2 oranges*
1 lemon	*1 lemon*

1. Break the bay leaves into small pieces. With a sharp knife point, make slits in the fish skin and insert the pieces of bay leaf under the skin.
2. Brush olive oil over the fish and season with salt and pepper. Place the fish on a rack set over a pan of water and transfer to a preheated moderate oven (180°C/350°F, Gas Mark 4) for 20 minutes.
3. Meanwhile, peel the oranges and lemon and section them over a saucepan to catch the juice. Add the fruit segments and a tablespoon of olive oil to the saucepan and heat the mixture gently for 2 to 3 minutes.
4. Transfer the fish to a warm serving dish and spoon over the orange and lemon sauce.

Trout in White Vermouth

METRIC/IMPERIAL	AMERICAN
4 fresh trout	*4 fresh lake trout*
2 onions, chopped	*2 onions, chopped*
120 ml/4 fl oz white vermouth	*½ cup white vermouth*

1. Clean the fish, leaving on their heads and tails.
2. Place each trout on a piece of foil large enough to form a closed package around it, or in a roasting bag. Sauté the onions briefly in butter and divide them between the trout.
3. Pour a few tablespoons of fish stock and a quarter of the vermouth over each fish, and season with salt and pepper.
4. Fold the edges of the foil over and press together to make loose, closed packages. Put the packages in a preheated moderate oven (180°C/350°F, Gas Mark 4) for about 15 minutes. After this time, open one of the packages to see if the fish is cooked. Return to the oven for a few minutes, if necessary, then serve.

Baked Red Mullet with Citrus Fruit: be sure to use red, not grey, mullet – there's a world of difference between them.

Salt Cod de Brix

METRIC/IMPERIAL	AMERICAN
1 kg/2 lb salt cod	*2 lb salt cod*
750 g/1½ lb onions, sliced	*1½ lb onions, sliced*
1 kg/2 lb potatoes, scrubbed	*2 lb potatoes, scrubbed*
175 ml/6 fl oz single cream	*¾ cup light cream*

1. Soak the cod in cold water for 4 to 6 hours to remove the salt. You will need to change the water once or twice.
2. When all the salt is removed, put the cod in a saucepan and cover with fresh cold water; bring to the boil. Reduce the heat and simmer very gently for about 20 minutes.
3. In the meantime, sauté the onions in butter over low heat until they are transparent. In another pan, boil the potatoes in their skins until they are just soft. Drain and cut into round slices.
4. Remove the skin and bones from the cod and place it in an ovenproof dish. Arrange the onion and potato slices over the fish. Pour the cream over and place the dish in a preheated moderately hot oven (190°C/375°F, Gas Mark 5) for about 20 minutes, until the top is golden brown. Serve immediately.

Soused Herring

METRIC/IMPERIAL	AMERICAN
1 onion, sliced	*1 onion, sliced*
4 herring, filleted	*4 herring, filleted*
2 bay leaves	*2 bay leaves*
125 ml/4 fl oz wine vinegar	*½ cup wine vinegar*

1. Place a slice of onion on each of the fillets and roll them up, with the skin on the outside. Spear each of the rolls through with a cocktail stick (toothpick) to hold them together.
2. Put the rolls in an ovenproof casserole with the bay leaves, a few peppercorns and any leftover onion.
3. Pour over the vinegar and enough water just to cover the fish. Cover and cook over low heat for 1½ hours.
4. Transfer the rolls to a deep serving dish. Strain the cooking liquid and pour this over the fish. Allow to cool and then place in the refrigerator. Serve when the liquid has turned to jelly.

Soused Herring: in the old days sousing was a way of preserving herring. Now it's a favourite way of preparing them.

Golden Fish

METRIC/IMPERIAL	AMERICAN
1 kg/2 lb carrots, coarsely grated	*5 cups coarsely grated carrots*
500 g/1 lb onions, chopped	*4 cups chopped onions*
1 whole firm white fish (about 1.75 kg/4 lb), cleaned	*1 whole firm white fish (about 4 lb), cleaned*
juice of one lemon	*juice of 1 lemon*

1. Sauté the carrots and onions together in three tablespoons each of butter and oil until just tender. Season to taste with salt and pepper.
2. Place about one third of the carrot and onion mixture in a buttered baking dish. Season the fish inside and out with salt and pepper, then lay it on the bed of onion and carrot. Mound the rest of the mixture over and around the fish and sprinkle with the lemon juice.
3. Transfer the dish to a preheated moderate oven (180°C/350°F, Gas Mark 4) for approximately 45 minutes. Partially cover with a piece of foil if the vegetables are in danger of burning.
4. Push aside the vegetable mixture and remove the skin from the top and sides of the fish, leaving the head intact. Replace the carrot and onion mixture and serve.

Lebanese Charcoal Chicken

METRIC/IMPERIAL	AMERICAN
2 small young chickens	2 small young chickens
10 garlic cloves	10 garlic cloves
1 tablespoon lemon juice	1 tablespoon lemon juice

1. Clean the chickens and cut each in half.
2. Grill the chicken halves for 10 to 15 minutes each side on a charcoal grill.
3. As it cooks, brush the meat from time to time with olive oil, and sprinkle with salt and pepper to taste.
4. Peel the garlic and pound it in a mortar and pestle. Add to it 1 teaspoon salt, 2 tablespoons olive oil and the lemon juice and stir until the mixture is smooth. Using a small brush, spread the sauce over the chicken and continue cooking until crispy. Transfer to dinner plates and serve immediately.

Roast Chicken Flambé

METRIC/IMPERIAL	AMERICAN
1 × 1.5 kg/3 lb chicken	1 × 3 lb chicken
125 g/4 oz cottage cheese or Petit Suisse (cream cheese)	½ cup cottage cheese or Petit Suisse (cream cheese)
1 to 2 sprigs fresh tarragon or 2 teaspoons dried	1 to 2 sprigs fresh tarragon or 2 teaspoons dried
8–10 tablespoons whisky	½–⅔ cup whisky

1. Wipe the chicken and rub it with butter, inside and out.
2. Spoon the cottage cheese and tarragon into the chicken. Sprinkle the outside with salt and pepper.
3. Place the chicken on its side, on a rack set over a roasting pan and roast in a preheated moderately hot oven (200°C/400°F, Gas Mark 6); after 20 minutes, turn it over for a further 20 minutes, then turn it breast side up for a final 20 minutes or until cooked. Remove the chicken from the oven, and flambé it with half of the whisky.
4. Place the chicken on a hot platter. Reduce the pan juices over high heat for a couple of minutes, then pour the whisky sauce over the chicken and take to the table. Flambé again with the remaining whisky and carve.

Lemon Chicken

METRIC/IMPERIAL	AMERICAN
1 × 1.5 kg/3 lb chicken or 8 chicken pieces	1 × 3 lb chicken or 8 chicken pieces
6 tablespoons lemon juice	6 tablespoons lemon juice
200 g/7 oz long-grain rice	1 cup long-grain rice
2 tablespoons sautéed pine nuts	2 tablespoons sautéed pine nuts (pignoli)

1. Butter an ovenproof pan or baking dish. Cut the whole chicken into eight pieces (wings, legs and each breast cut in half).
2. Put the chicken pieces in the pan and sprinkle them with the lemon juice. Season with salt and pepper and dot with knobs of unsalted (sweet) butter.
3. Cook the chicken in a preheated hot oven (220°C/425°F, Gas Mark 7) for 1 hour, then turn off the heat and allow it to stand in the oven for another 10 minutes. Meanwhile, cook the rice according to the instructions on the packet, or until tender, then drain and stir in the pine nuts (pignoli).
4. When the chicken is cooked, remove the dish from the oven and reserve the pan juices. Skim off the surplus butter, spoon the juices over the chicken and serve.

NOTE: This dish may be served hot or cold; if left overnight in the refrigerator, the chicken becomes deliciously jellied!

Roast Chicken Flambé: flaming is always spectacular, but be sure you step back from the dish or you may lose an eyebrow!

Sesame Chicken

METRIC/IMPERIAL	AMERICAN
4 boneless chicken breasts	4 boneless chicken breasts
4 tablespoons soy sauce	¼ cup soy sauce
2 tablespoons lemon juice and 4 slices of lemon	2 tablespoons lemon juice and 4 slices of lemon
8 tablespoons toasted sesame seeds	8 tablespoons toasted sesame seeds

1. Marinate the chicken breasts for 30 minutes to 1 hour in half the soy sauce, the lemon juice and 2 tablespoons warm water. Turn the chicken in the marinade from time to time so that all the meat is covered.
2. Discard the marinade. Roll the chicken breasts in the sesame seeds, and place a slice of lemon on each breast.
3. Lay the chicken pieces flat and slightly apart in a roasting bag. Distribute the remaining soy sauce over them and tie up the bag.
4. Place the bag on a baking sheet and bake in a preheated moderate oven (180°C/350°F, Gas Mark 4) for 30 to 35 minutes. To serve, remove the chicken breasts from the roasting bag and pour over the juices.

Chicken Basquaise

METRIC/IMPERIAL	AMERICAN
12 oz long-grain rice	1¾ cups long-grain rice
4 chicken breasts on the bone	4 chicken breasts on the bone
1 kg/2 lb tomatoes, skinned	2 lb tomatoes, peeled
2 chillies, finely chopped	2 chilies, finely chopped

Also have ready: *350 ml/12 fl oz (1½ cups) chicken stock*

1. Cook the rice in the chicken stock for about 20 minutes, until it is just tender but not soft.
2. Melt some butter in a casserole and brown the chicken breasts on both sides; add salt and pepper to taste.
3. Cover the chicken with the rice.
4. Cut the tomatoes in wedges and mix them with the chillies. Place them on top of the rice and bake, covered, in a preheated moderately hot oven (200°C/400°F, Gas Mark 6) for 30 minutes, or until the tomatoes are soft and the meat tender.

Sesame Chicken: like Aladdin's secret phrase, sesame can turn ordinary fare into something magical.

Chicken Baked in a Salt Crust

METRIC/IMPERIAL	AMERICAN
1 × 1.5 kg/3 lb chicken (with its liver)	1 × 3 lb chicken (with its liver)
6 garlic cloves	6 garlic cloves
2 sprigs fresh rosemary or 1 teaspoon dried rosemary	2 sprigs fresh rosemary or 1 teaspoon dried rosemary
1 kg/2 lb flour	8 cups flour

Also have ready: *500 g/1 lb (1⅓ cups) sea salt*

1. Clean the chicken thoroughly, season inside with pepper and put the liver, garlic and rosemary into the cavity.
2. Mix together the flour, sea salt and 500 ml/18 fl oz (2¼ cups) water to a thick paste. Spread the paste all around the outside of the chicken so that it is completely sealed – do this with a wet spoon, as the paste is extremely heavy and sticky.
3. Place the coated chicken in a baking dish and cook in a preheated hot oven (220°C/425°F, Gas Mark 7) for 1¼ hours.
4. Take the chicken from the oven and break the coating open with a heavy ladle. Transfer the chicken to a serving plate and carve it in the usual way.

Silver Chicken

METRIC/IMPERIAL	AMERICAN
1 × 1.5 kg/3 lb chicken	1 × 3 lb chicken
1 onion, chopped	1 onion, chopped
1 bouquet garni	1 bouquet garni
4 to 5 tablespoons fresh chopped tarragon	4 to 5 tablespoons fresh chopped tarragon

1. Fill the cavity of the chicken with as many spoons or forks, preferably silver, as it will hold. These are very good conductors of heat.
2. Place the chicken in a saucepan which is just large enough to hold it, and just cover with cold water. Add the chopped onion, bouquet garni and tarragon.
3. Bring to the boil and allow to boil rapidly for five minutes only. Turn off the heat and leave the chicken in the water, covered, for 2 to 3 hours. The heat retained by the spoons will continue to cook the chicken.
4. Remove the spoons before serving. The chicken flesh is very juicy and full of flavour and can be served with vegetables or salad, or used in pies and sandwiches.

Roast Duck with Honey and Mustard

METRIC/IMPERIAL	AMERICAN
1.75 kg/4 lb duck	4 lb duck
juice of 1 lemon	juice of 1 lemon
1½ tablespoons dry mustard	1½ tablespoons dry mustard
4 tablespoons honey	4 tablespoons honey

1. Rub the duck with salt, pepper and lemon juice inside and out. Prick the skin in several places to allow the fat to escape.
2. Place the duck on a rack set over a roasting pan and place in a preheated moderate oven (160°C/325°F, Gas Mark 3) for 1 hour; excess fat will be caught in the pan.
3. Meanwhile, make a basting mixture by combining the mustard and honey. At the end of the cooking time, brush the meat with this mixture and repeat every 10 minutes or so. Cook the duck for a further 30 minutes until fairly well done.
4. Using poultry shears, cut the duck into four portions and serve.

NOTE: Alternatively, cook on a spit for the same length of time.

Roast Duck in Champagne

METRIC/IMPERIAL	AMERICAN
1 × 1.75 kg/4 lb duck, with its liver	1 × 4 lb duck, with its liver
2 shallots, chopped	2 shallots, chopped
½ bottle champagne	½ bottle champagne
2 to 3 tablespoons cognac	2 to 3 tablespoons cognac

1. Prepare the duck by first roasting it in a preheated hot oven (230°C/450°F, Gas Mark 8) for about 30 minutes, leaving it just underdone. Cut off the breast and slice into narrow strips; cut off the legs and wings. Grill (broil) the legs for about 10 minutes more under medium heat. Arrange all the duck portions in a serving dish and keep hot.
2. Remove the rest of the meat from the carcass and chop it. In a frying pan (skillet), melt 50 g/2 oz (¼ cup) butter and sauté the chopped meat with the shallots; add salt and pepper to taste.
3. Pour the champagne into the pan and reduce it by half. Then press the sauce through a sieve (strainer). Return it to the pan and thicken with the duck's liver (also passed through the sieve), and 2 tablespoons of butter.
4. Finally, stir the cognac into the sauce and reheat. To serve, coat the duck pieces with the sauce.

Roast Duck with Honey and Mustard:
an unusual combination that produces a delicious result.

Pigeon Parcels

METRIC/IMPERIAL	AMERICAN
a handful of tarragon sprigs	*a handful of tarragon sprigs*
4 pigeons, cleaned	*4 pigeons, cleaned*
500 g/1 lb sliced bacon	*1 lb bacon slices*
4 slices bread	*4 slices bread*

1. Place 6 to 8 sprigs of tarragon in the cavity of each pigeon.
2. Divide the bacon into four equal parts and cover each bird with the slices; tie them onto the birds.
3. Lay the birds in a baking dish on their sides and sprinkle with olive oil, salt and pepper to taste. Put the pigeons in a preheated moderately hot oven (200°C/400°F, Gas Mark 6) for 15 minutes. Turn the birds and return to the oven for a further 10 minutes.
4. Fry the bread in olive oil or butter. Remove the string and place each pigeon on a slice of fried bread to serve.

Squab with Sage and Bacon

METRIC/IMPERIAL	AMERICAN
4 squab (young pigeon bred especially for the table), with livers (optional)	*4 squab (young pigeon bred especially for the table), with livers (optional)*
30 fresh sage leaves	*30 fresh sage leaves*
4 rashers back bacon	*4 slices Canadian bacon*
125 ml/4 fl oz red wine	*½ cup red wine*

1. Wash the squab in cold water and dry them both inside and out. Stuff each cavity with 3 to 4 sage leaves, a slice of bacon and, if liked, a liver; add salt and pepper to taste.
2. In a frying pan (skillet) large enough to hold all four birds, melt 3 tablespoons butter in the same amount of olive oil. When it is hot, add the remaining sage leaves and brown the squab.
3. Add the wine and boil it for 30 seconds, using it to baste the birds as it boils. Lower the heat, cover the frying pan (skillet) and continue cooking, basting the birds every 15 minutes, for an hour. Add a little more wine or stock if necessary.
4. When cooked, transfer the squab to a warmed platter. Add a little water to the pan and scrape the juices into a gravy to pour over the birds, and serve.

Pigeon Parcels: "Pigeons in the grass alas," wailed Gertrude Stein, but surely she would have appreciated these.

Sautéed Quail in Vine Leaves

METRIC/IMPERIAL	AMERICAN
8 fresh vine leaves	*8 fresh vine leaves*
8 quail, cleaned	*8 quail, cleaned*
8 rashers unsmoked bacon	*8 unsmoked bacon slices*
120 ml/4 fl oz dry white wine	*½ cup dry white wine*

Also have ready: *120 ml/4 fl oz (½ cup) olive oil*

1. If you cannot obtain fresh vine leaves, Greek and specialist food shops sell them preserved in brine. Wash either type, especially preserved leaves, carefully in cold water; or blanch them quickly in boiling water and then dip them in cold water. Drain the leaves well.
2. Sprinkle the insides of the quail with a generous pinch of salt and pepper; add a large knob of butter. Wrap a vine leaf around each bird, then a slice of bacon, and tie this wrapping on with string. Brush the quail with melted butter.
3. Place the eight birds in a flameproof baking dish with a lid. Heat the olive oil in the dish on top of the stove and sauté the quail for 3 minutes to brown slightly. Add the wine, cover the dish and simmer over a low heat for 45 minutes.
4. During the last 30 minutes of cooking, baste the quail frequently with the juices, replacing the lid between bastings. When they are cooked, transfer the quail to a serving platter and cut off the strings. Pour a spoonful of cooking liquid over each bird, and serve immediately.

Partridge with Grapes

METRIC/IMPERIAL	AMERICAN
8 rashers fat bacon	8 fat bacon slices
4 partridges, cleaned	4 partridges, cleaned
1 bouquet garni	1 bouquet garni
1 kg/2 lb white seedless grapes, peeled	2 lb white seedless grapes, peeled

1. Lay 2 slices of bacon on each partridge and tie with string.
2. Gently heat the remaining bacon in a large casserole until the fat begins to run. Add the bouquet garni, the partridges, and the grapes piled on and around the partridges. Place a knob of butter on each bird, and add salt and pepper to taste.
3. Cover the casserole and simmer gently for 1 hour, basting the partridges occasionally. Add a little stock or water as necessary.
4. When the birds are cooked, snip off the string. Serve the birds accompanied by the bacon and grapes.

Partridge Casserole with Brandy

METRIC/IMPERIAL	AMERICAN
4 partridges, cleaned	4 partridges, cleaned
250 g/8 oz cream cheese	1 cup cream cheese
8 bacon rashers	8 bacon slices
120 ml/4 fl oz cognac	½ cup cognac

Also have ready: 125 g/4 oz (½ cup) butter

1. Fill the cavities of the birds as full as possible with the cream cheese, and fasten the openings with skewers or cocktail sticks (toothpicks). Lay two slices of bacon over each bird and tie this on with string.
2. In a very large flameproof casserole, melt the butter. When it is hot, put in the birds. Season with salt and pepper to taste. Cover the casserole and cook over a low heat for 30 minutes, basting occasionally with the juices.
3. Cut the strings and remove the bacon from the birds, then increase the heat and brown them on all sides in the pan juices. Continue cooking for 15 minutes with the lid on.
4. Transfer the partridges to a serving platter and keep them hot. Pour the cognac into the casserole and deglaze it, stirring and scraping the sides and bottom to dissolve the meaty residues and form a sauce. Pour the sauce over the partridges and serve.

Roast Pheasant

METRIC/IMPERIAL	AMERICAN
2 small pheasants, cleaned	2 small pheasants, cleaned
6 to 8 rashers bacon	6 to 8 bacon slices
4 slices toast	4 slices toast
4 slices pâté de foie gras (optional)	4 slices pâté de foie gras (optional)

1. Pheasants are best hung briefly – not more than 4 to 6 days. Often the butcher has prepared them ready for the oven, with a piece of pork fat tied around them; cut this off, as the birds are tastier wrapped with bacon. Wipe the pheasants well with a damp cloth or paper towel.
2. Rub softened butter all over the pheasants and sprinkle with salt and pepper. Lay the slices of bacon over them and tie them on with string.
3. Arrange the birds on a rack and place the slices of toast in the roasting pan underneath them to catch the cooking juices.
4. Cook the pheasants in a preheated moderate oven (180°C/350°F, Gas Mark 4) for about 45 minutes (allow 15 to 20 minutes per 500 g/1 lb). Remove the bacon and cut the pheasants in half along the breastbone. Place each half on a piece of toast and arrange on a large serving platter. If desired, serve each pheasant with a slice of pâté de foie gras on top.

Partridge with Grapes: handle partridges with care as overcooking can toughen their delicate flesh.

GOOD COMPANIONS

The French usually serve vegetables as a separate course. This admirable custom allows their delicate flavours to be savoured and appreciated to the full. On the other hand, many vegetable dishes make excellent accompaniments to meat, fish and poultry, enhancing their flavour and adding colour and variety to the meal.

Whether as accompaniments or independent items, vegetables should always be lightly cooked to preserve their freshness. Properly prepared and beautifully presented, these good companions should give vegetables a well deserved boost up the socio-gastronomic ladder.

Broad Bean Tortilla

METRIC/IMPERIAL	AMERICAN
125 g/4 oz small shelled broad beans	⅔ cup small hulled fava beans
6 eggs	6 eggs

1. Clean the beans, removing the bitter sproutings, and sauté them in olive oil in a large frying pan (skillet) over a high heat for 5 minutes.
2. Whisk the eggs lightly with a fork and add salt and pepper.
3. Pour the eggs over the beans, stir to distribute them evenly and cook slowly until the tortilla has browned on the bottom and set.
4. Invert the tortilla onto a serving platter, and pour any oil left in the pan over the top to give an attractive finish. Grind a little fresh pepper over the surface. This 'omelette' can be made in advance and served at room temperature.

French Beans in Paprika Sauce

METRIC/IMPERIAL	AMERICAN
500 g/1 lb young green beans	1 lb young green beans
1 bunch spring onions, with their green tops	1 bunch scallions, with their green tops
150 ml/¼ pint soured cream	⅔ cup sour cream
1 tablespoon paprika	1 tablespoon paprika

1. Prepare the beans by cutting off their stems and tails. Cook them in a saucepan of boiling, salted water for 10 to 12 minutes or until they are just tender, taking care not to overcook. Drain the beans and return them to the pan.
2. Clean, slice and chop the spring onions (scallions). Cook them in a little olive oil over a medium heat for about 4 minutes, then add to the beans.
3. Warm the soured cream in a small pan over low heat. Stir in the paprika and a pinch of salt (you can adjust the quantity of paprika to suit your taste).
4. Heat the vegetables through over low heat, taking care not to boil, and serve with the sauce poured over.

French Beans in Paprika Sauce: if you can find it, use fresh Hungarian paprika in this dish. Your tongue will notice!

Polish Style Cauliflower

METRIC/IMPERIAL	AMERICAN
2 medium cauliflowers	2 medium heads cauliflower
3 hard-boiled eggs, sliced	3 hard-cooked eggs, sliced
juice of 2 lemons	juice of 2 lemons
50 g/2 oz fresh breadcrumbs, toasted	1 cup soft bread crumbs, toasted

Also have ready: 125 g/4 oz (½ cup) butter

1. Wash the cauliflowers and remove the outside leaves and stems; separate them into florets. Boil the florets in salted water for about 15 minutes until tender.
2. Drain the florets well and pack them tightly into a bowl just large enough to accommodate them and act as a mould. Allow to stand for a few minutes.
3. Turn the mound of cauliflower out onto a flat dish, and arrange the slices of egg around the edge.
4. Melt the butter and coat the mound with it. Pour the lemon juice over the mound, and finally sprinkle over the toasted breadcrumbs. Be sure that each person served gets a fair share of the butter, lemon and crumbs!

Marina's Cauliflower

METRIC/IMPERIAL	AMERICAN
1 handful fresh, chopped parsley	1 handful fresh, chopped parsley
2 garlic cloves, chopped	2 garlic cloves, chopped
2 cauliflowers, broken into florets	2 heads cauliflower, broken into florets
3 teaspoons tomato purée	3 teaspoons tomato paste

1. Warm a little olive oil in a frying pan (skillet) and cook the parsley and garlic until they are warmed through, but do not let the garlic colour. Add a tablespoon of water to the pan.
2. Toss the cauliflower florets in the pan until they are well covered by the oil, parsley and garlic.
3. Melt the tomato purée (paste) in 125 ml/4 fl oz (½ cup) warm water and gradually stir this into the cauliflower; add salt and pepper to taste.
4. Stew gently until the cauliflower is cooked but still slightly crisp; serve immediately.

French Style Broad Beans

METRIC/IMPERIAL	AMERICAN
1.75 kg/4 lb broad beans, shelled	4 lb fava beans, hulled
250 g/8 oz pickling onions, peeled	½ lb pearl onions, peeled
150 g/5 oz cooked ham, cut into strips	5 oz cooked ham, cut into strips
1 tablespoon dried summer savory	1 tablespoon dried summer savory

1. Boil 2.25 litres/4 pints (10 cups) water, add the beans and bring the water back to the boil. Turn off the heat, allow the beans to rest for 5 minutes, then tip them into a colander and refresh them under cold running water. Drain the beans.
2. Skin the beans by making a little cut in the stalk side and pressing the skin to pop the bean out.
3. Dry the saucepan and melt 2 tablespoons butter in it. Add the onions, the ham and the savory. Cook these over a low heat for 20 minutes, stirring frequently, then add the beans and 5 tablespoons hot water. Season the beans lightly with salt and pepper.
4. Cook the beans over a medium heat (to keep them whole) for about 10 minutes, turning them from time to time. Just before serving, reduce the juice, if necessary, over a high heat. Add a further 2 tablespoons butter to the beans and stir in.

Polish Style Cauliflower: an Eastern European recipe that improves the usually rather banal taste of cauliflower.

Mushrooms in Coaches

METRIC/IMPERIAL	AMERICAN
500 g / 1 lb mushrooms, sliced	1 lb mushrooms, sliced
1 tablespoon flour	1 tablespoon flour
4 × 4 cm / 1½ inch thick slices white bread	4 × 1½ inch thick slices white bread
75 ml / 2 fl oz single cream	¼ cup light cream

Also have ready: 50 g / 2 oz (¼ cup) clarified butter

1. Cook the mushrooms in butter over a low heat for about 20 minutes, or until they become quite black. Sprinkle them with the flour, stir and cook for a further 2 minutes.
2. Slice the crusts off the bread to leave eight 10 cm / 4 inch squares. Leaving a 1.25 cm / ½ inch border, cut a square well in the centre of each slice to a depth of 2.5 cm / 1 inch. Remove the bread from the centre. Fry each of these 'coaches' on all sides in the clarified butter until they are golden. Keep the bread warm.
3. Mix the cream with the mushrooms to bind them loosely together. Salt and pepper the mixture generously.
4. Warm the mushrooms and cream through gently, and spoon into the hollows in the 'coaches'; serve immediately.

Whisky Carrots

METRIC/IMPERIAL	AMERICAN
500 g / 1 lb carrots	1 lb carrots
1 tablespoon lemon juice	1 tablespoon lemon juice
2 tablespoons sugar	2 tablespoons sugar
4 tablespoons whisky	¼ cup whisky

Also have ready: 125 g / 4 oz (½ cup) softened butter

1. Slice the carrots thinly and parboil them in salted water.
2. Put them in a baking dish with the lemon juice, sugar, whisky and butter. Stir everything together and add pepper to taste.
3. Cover the dish and cook in a preheated moderate oven (180°C/ 350°F, Gas Mark 4) for about 1 hour, stirring occasionally.
4. At the end of cooking, remove the carrots from the oven; they should be deliciously caramelized.

Mushrooms in Coaches: mushrooms don't usually arrive in coaches, but when they do they arrive succulently!

Potatoes au Gratin

METRIC/IMPERIAL	AMERICAN
1.5 kg / 3 lb potatoes, peeled	3 lb potatoes, peeled
250 ml / 8 fl oz single cream	1 cup light cream
120 ml / 4 fl oz milk	½ cup milk
75 g / 3 oz Gruyère cheese, grated	¾ cup grated Gruyère cheese

1. Parboil the potatoes, slice them thinly and pat dry.
2. Spread a thin layer of cream on the bottom of a large baking dish. Arrange the potatoes and cheese in alternate layers in the baking dish, saving some of the cheese for a topping, and sprinkle with salt and pepper. Finally, add the remaining cream and milk to cover the potatoes.
3. Cover the dish with foil and stand it in a bain-marie. Place this in a preheated moderate oven (180°C/350°F, Gas Mark 4) for about 45 minutes, or until the potatoes are cooked. Remove the foil and replace the dish in the oven to brown. Add more cream or milk if the potatoes seem to be drying out.
4. Sprinkle the top with the rest of the cheese, and place under a hot grill (broiler) for 2 to 3 minutes until crisp and golden. Serve immediately.

Potato Dauphinois

METRIC/IMPERIAL	AMERICAN
600 ml / 1 pint milk	2½ cups milk
1 egg	1 egg
1 garlic clove	1 garlic clove
1 kg / 2 lb potatoes	2 lb potatoes

1. Beat the milk and egg together in a bowl and add salt and pepper to taste.
2. Rub the garlic all around a shallow, ovenproof dish then dot with softened butter and spread it evenly. Peel the potatoes and slice them very finely.
3. Place the potato slices in neat lines in the buttered dish, one layer on top of the other, pouring egg and milk mixture between each layer. Dot the top layer with a few knobs of butter.
4. Bake the potatoes in a preheated moderately hot oven (190°C/ 375°F, Gas Mark 5) for 1½ hours or until the potatoes are soft, and the surface golden brown.

Hot and Cold Salad

METRIC/IMPERIAL	AMERICAN
6 to 8 celery sticks	6 to 8 stalks celery
1 green and 1 red pepper	1 green and 1 red pepper
1 tablespoon wine vinegar	1 tablespoon wine vinegar
8 lettuce leaves	8 lettuce leaves

Also have ready: 5 tablespoons olive oil

1. Wash the celery, removing any tough fibres, and chop it into 1.5 cm/½ inch pieces.
2. Slice the peppers lengthwise into approximately 2.5 cm/1 inch wide strips, removing all seeds and membranes. Place the strips under a grill (broiler) for about 5 minutes, with their outer sides up, until some of them scorch. Cut them into smaller sections, about 4 cm/1½ inches long.
3. Mix the olive oil with the vinegar and season with salt and pepper to taste to make a vinaigrette dressing.
4. While the peppers are still hot, toss them with the celery and the vinaigrette, and serve on the lettuce leaves.

Peperonata

METRIC/IMPERIAL	AMERICAN
250 g/8 oz onions, chopped	½ lb onions, chopped
500 g/1 lb red peppers	1 lb red peppers
500 g/1 lb ripe tomatoes	1 lb ripe tomatoes
1 garlic clove, chopped	1 garlic clove, chopped

1. Cook the onions in 3 tablespoons olive oil until they are translucent.
2. Core and seed the peppers and slice them into strips. Add them to the onions, with salt to taste, and simmer, covered, for 15 minutes.
3. Peel, quarter and seed the tomatoes and add to the onions with the garlic.
4. Cook the mixture slowly for 15 minutes more, then serve.

NOTE: A mixture of green, red and yellow peppers produces a colourful dish. If desired, you can substitute four chopped anchovy fillets for the garlic.

Ratatouille

METRIC/IMPERIAL	AMERICAN
2 aubergines	2 eggplant
2 red or green peppers	2 red or green peppers
2 large onions, sliced	2 large onions, sliced
4 tomatoes, skinned and chopped	4 tomatoes, peeled and chopped

Also have ready: 175 ml/6 fl oz (¾ cup) olive oil

1. Cut the aubergines (eggplant) into 2.5 cm/1 inch cubes. Prepare the peppers by taking out the core, seeds and white ribs, then dicing them. Mixing green and red peppers adds a bit of colour.
2. Heat the olive oil in a large saucepan and cook the onions until they are transparent.
3. Add the peppers to the pan, then the aubergines and continue to cook over a low heat for 10 minutes. At the end of this time, add the tomatoes.
4. Cover the pan and simmer the ratatouille for 30 minutes. Take the lid off and continue to simmer over a very low heat for another 10 minutes – the vegetables should stew, not fry, in the oil. Serve hot or cold.

Riboon

METRIC/IMPERIAL	AMERICAN
500 g/1 lb tomatoes	1 lb tomatoes
2 avocados	2 avocados
1 garlic clove	1 garlic clove
8 slices toast or 12 slices French bread, lightly fried in clarified butter	8 slices toast or 12 slices French bread, lightly fried in clarified butter

1. Peel and roughly chop the tomatoes. Halve and peel the avocados and chop them into small pieces.
2. Mince the garlic finely.
3. Toss the tomatoes, avocados and garlic together in a bowl with 2 tablespoons olive oil, and add salt and pepper to taste.
4. To serve, pile the mixture onto the toast (with the crusts removed) or fried French bread.

Hot and Cold Salad: a crunchy salad that's
true to its name. Remove the scorched patches if you prefer.

Sweet and Sour Onions

METRIC/IMPERIAL	AMERICAN
500 g/1 lb pickling onions	1 lb pearl onions
2 bay leaves	2 bay leaves
1 teaspoon sugar	1 teaspoon sugar
2 tablespoons wine vinegar	2 tablespoons wine vinegar

1. Buy tiny onions, 2.5 cm/1 inch or less in diameter if possible, or small shallots. Halved, ordinary onions are equally delicious, but do not look as attractive.
2. Cook the onions, unpeeled, in boiling salted water for 10 to 15 minutes until tender; leave them to cool.
3. Dry the onions and peel them. Dry the saucepan, add 2 tablespoons olive oil, the bay leaves and the onions and simmer over a very low heat for 5 minutes, stirring occasionally.
4. Add the sugar and vinegar to the onions; discard the bay leaves. Test the flavour and add more sugar or vinegar if necessary. Continue to cook the onions, stirring, for another minute or so, until the sauce turns syrupy. Serve the onions either hot or cold.

Mulled Chestnuts

METRIC/IMPERIAL	AMERICAN
750 g/1½ lb peeled chestnuts	1½ lb peeled chestnuts
6 tablespoons port	6 tablespoons port
1 small onion stuck with 2 cloves	1 small onion stuck with 2 cloves

Also have ready: 750 ml//1¾ pints (4¼ cups) chicken stock and 75 g/3 oz (⅓ cup) butter

1. Make a little cut in each chestnut and boil for 5 minutes to loosen the inside skins. Cool and skin them, then cook again in boiling salted water for about 20 minutes.
2. Drain the chestnuts and place them in a saucepan with the chicken stock, the port and the onion stuck with cloves.
3. Add the butter to the pan and allow to simmer over a low heat for about 20 minutes. Remove the onion and discard.
4. Continue to cook over low heat, stirring carefully so as not to break up the chestnuts, until the liquid has become syrupy and the chestnuts are well coated. Serve immediately.

Mulled Chestnuts: chestnuts are fairly hardy, they can be shelled, peeled, cooked in advance and set aside until needed.

Jack and Joan's Courgettes

METRIC/IMPERIAL	AMERICAN
8 small courgettes	8 small zucchini
2 teaspoons dried oregano	2 teaspoons dried oregano
125 g/4 oz Parmesan cheese, coarsely grated	1 cup coarsely grated Parmesan cheese
50 g/2 oz dried breadcrumbs or savoury biscuit crumbs	½ cup dry bread crumbs or cracker crumbs

1. Cut the courgettes (zucchini) in half lengthwise and score the cut sides with a sharp knife. Place the courgettes in a baking pan and spread them with softened butter.
2. Sprinkle the courgettes with the oregano, the Parmesan and salt and pepper to taste.
3. Top the whole affair with the crumbs.
4. Place under a medium hot grill (broiler) for 20 minutes, or until the dish is very crusty and brown on top.

Mini Courgette Pancakes

METRIC/IMPERIAL	AMERICAN
1 kg/2 lb courgettes	2 lb zucchini
75 g/3 oz self-raising flour	¾ cup self-rising flour
1 egg, lightly beaten	1 egg, lightly beaten
75 g/3 oz Parmesan cheese, grated	¾ cup grated Parmesan cheese

1. Grate the courgettes (zucchini) onto a clean kitchen towel, wrap the towel around them and wring it to squeeze out their natural moisture.
2. In a large mixing bowl, combine the dry courgettes with the flour and egg. Season with salt and pepper to taste. Mix together thoroughly.
3. Melt plenty of clarified butter in a large frying pan (skillet) and drop in spoonfuls of the courgette mixture to form as many small (5 cm/2 inch) pancakes as you have room for in the pan. Fry the pancakes in two batches if necessary.
4. Brown the pancakes lightly on both sides, then remove them from the heat and brush them with a little of the melted clarified butter. Sprinkle them with the Parmesan cheese and serve immediately.

Braised Fennel

METRIC/IMPERIAL	AMERICAN
2 tablespoons flour	*2 tablespoons flour*
8 small bulbs fennel or 4 large bulbs, halved	*8 small bulbs fennel or 4 large bulbs, halved*
juice of 1 lemon	*juice of 1 lemon*
2 tablespoons chopped chives	*2 teaspoons chopped chives*

1. Bring to the boil a large pan of salted water, sprinkle in the flour and stir it into the water (this is to keep the fennel white). Drop in the fennel and cook until just tender.
2. Test the fennel with a fork, taking care not to overcook it. Remove the fennel from the pan and refresh in cold water. Cut the bulbs into quarters, drain them well and pat dry.
3. Melt 3 tablespoons butter in the pan and sauté the fennel over a very low heat for about 5 minutes.
4. Pepper the fennel lightly and stir in the lemon juice. Cover the pan and simmer for a further 5 minutes. Sprinkle the chives over the top and serve.

Creamed Cabbage

METRIC/IMPERIAL	AMERICAN
1 medium green cabbage	*1 medium head green cabbage*
2 cooking apples	*2 tart apples*
150 ml/¼ pint soured cream	*⅔ cup sour cream*
1 tablespoon caraway seeds	*1 tablespoon caraway seeds*

1. Cut out the cabbage core, then shred the cabbage finely. Sweat it in butter (or bacon fat, if you prefer) for 5 minutes to partially cook.
2. Core and peel the apples, then slice them and cut the slices into strips; add these to the cabbage.
3. Mix the cream into the cabbage and apples and cook over a low heat for 15 minutes, stirring occasionally. The cabbage should be tender but not mushy.
4. Transfer the cabbage to a warmed serving dish and sprinkle with the caraway seeds. Serve the dish immediately.

Country Fried Cabbage

METRIC/IMPERIAL	AMERICAN
1 small white cabbage	*1 head small white cabbage*
3 to 4 rashers back bacon	*3 to 4 Canadian bacon slices*
300 ml/½ pint soured cream	*1¼ cups sour cream*

1. Remove and discard the stem and outside leaves of the cabbage, then shred it coarsely.
2. Fry the bacon in a large frying pan (skillet). When it is crisp, remove it, leaving the fat in the pan. Using a pair of wooden tongs or spatulas, stir-fry the cabbage in the fat, adding more if necessary, until it has wilted but is not soft. Keep the bacon warm.
3. Add the soured cream to the frying pan and cook over a low heat for a further 5 minutes, stirring occasionally.
4. Transfer the cabbage to a warmed serving dish. Grind some fresh pepper over it and add salt to taste. Crumble the bacon over the top and serve.

Braised Chicory

METRIC/IMPERIAL	AMERICAN
750 g/1½ lb chicory	*1½ lb endives*
1 teaspoon sugar	*1 teaspoon sugar*
250 g/8 oz sliced ham	*½ lb sliced ham*
juice of 1 lemon	*juice of 1 lemon*

1. Wash the chicory (endives) and remove the outside leaves, then slice them lengthwise and pat dry. Sauté them in 2 tablespoons each of butter and oil.
2. When the chicory becomes slightly browned, sprinkle on the sugar to caramelize them a little. Season with salt and pepper.
3. Wrap each piece of chicory in half a slice of ham. Put them in a flameproof casserole and sprinkle with the lemon juice. Cover the casserole and braise over a low heat for 30 minutes.
4. Before serving, take the lid off the casserole and reduce the liquid by rapidly boiling it for a few seconds.

Creamed Cabbage: an unusual dish which I recommend for its speed, simplicity and flavour.

Aubergines Baked with Tomatoes and Garlic

METRIC/IMPERIAL	AMERICAN
1 kg/2 lb aubergines	*2 lb eggplant*
1 × 350 g/12 oz can peeled Italian tomatoes	*1 × 12 oz can peeled Italian tomatoes*
1 garlic clove, crushed	*1 garlic clove, crushed*
thyme	*thyme*

1. Cut the aubergines (eggplant) into slices approximately 2.5 cm/1 inch thick. Salt the slices and set them aside for 30 minutes so that they give up some of their bitter juices.
2. Wipe the salt off the aubergines, and cut the slices into 2.5 cm/ 1 inch cubes.
3. In an ovenproof dish, combine the aubergines with the tomatoes, garlic, a pinch of thyme and salt and pepper to taste.
4. Bake the dish in a preheated moderate oven (180°C/350°F, Gas Mark 4) for about 35 to 40 minutes until the aubergines are cooked. Test to see that the aubergines are soft, then serve.

Baked Aubergine Slices

METRIC/IMPERIAL	AMERICAN
500 g/1 lb aubergines	*1 lb eggplant*

1. Slice the aubergines (eggplant) very thinly and sprinkle with salt to stop them from absorbing too much oil and to prevent bitterness.
2. Prepare a large baking dish by coating it with a thin layer of olive oil.
3. Place the aubergine slices side by side in the pan, touching each other but not overlapping. Brush them lightly with olive oil.
4. Bake the aubergines in a preheated moderate oven (180°C/ 350°F, Gas Mark 4) for 15 to 20 minutes, or until just soft. Turn the slices once so that both sides brown. Serve immediately.

Broccoli with Sesame Seeds: the superior broccoli is more cultivated than a cabbage and more robust than a cauliflower.

Turban of Aubergine

METRIC/IMPERIAL	AMERICAN
750 g/1½ lb aubergines	*1½ lb eggplant*
1 large garlic clove, crushed	*1 large garlic clove, crushed*
1 kg/2 lb tomatoes, peeled, chopped and seeded	*4 cups skinned, chopped and seeded tomatoes*
300 ml/½ pint plain yogurt	*1¼ cups plain yogurt*

1. Cut the aubergines (eggplant) into fine slices, salt them and set them aside for 30 minutes to allow the bitter juices to drain out. Pour off the juices, rinse the slices and pat them dry.
2. While the aubergines are still sweating, heat enough oil to cover the bottom of a saucepan. Add the garlic and then the tomatoes, and salt and pepper to taste. Cook the tomatoes for 15 to 20 minutes until they are soft. Stir 1 tablespoon butter into the sauce to give it a velvety texture and sheen.
3. In a separate pan, heat more olive oil and sauté the slices of aubergines on both sides until brown. Then arrange a layer of them on the bottom and around the sides of an ovenproof ring mould. Reserve a third of the tomato sauce. Arrange the remaining tomato sauce, the yogurt and the rest of the aubergine in layers.
4. Cover the dish, place in a preheated moderate oven (180°C/ 350°F, Gas Mark 4) and cook for about 45 minutes. Carefully turn the turban out onto a serving dish. Reheat the reserved tomato sauce and serve it with the turban.

Broccoli with Sesame Seeds

METRIC/IMPERIAL	AMERICAN
1 kg/2 lb broccoli	*2 lb broccoli*
75 g/3 oz sesame seeds, toasted	*½ cup sesame seeds, toasted*
3 tablespoons soy sauce	*3 tablespoons soy sauce*
4 tablespoons clear honey	*4 tablespoons clear honey*

1. Peel and trim the broccoli stalks, and break off the florets. Cut the stalks in half lengthwise, then into 2.5 cm/1 inch lengths.
2. Cook all the broccoli pieces in boiling salted water for about 10 minutes until they are tender but still crisp; drain and pat them dry with kitchen paper.
3. In a separate pan, stir the sesame seeds and soy sauce into the honey over a medium heat.
4. Reheat the broccoli by tossing it in a pan with a little hot oil. Transfer the broccoli to a serving dish and pour the sesame seed sauce over it.

Sweetcorn Soufflé

METRIC/IMPERIAL	AMERICAN
25 g/1 oz flour	4 tablespoons flour
500 ml/18 fl oz hot milk	2 cups hot milk
350 g/12 oz canned sweetcorn, drained	2 cups drained whole kernel corn
6 eggs, separated, yolks beaten	6 eggs, separated, yolks beaten

1. First, make a cream sauce: Melt 2 tablespoons butter in a saucepan over a low heat, then add the flour and blend well together. Stir this roux for 2 to 3 minutes.
2. Gradually add the hot milk to the roux, stirring constantly. Cook the sauce gently until smooth and creamy; continue stirring and season with salt and pepper to taste.
3. Empty the corn into the hot sauce. Stir for a minute, then reduce the heat and add the beaten egg yolks. Beat again for 1 to 2 minutes until the mixture thickens. Remove the pan from the heat and allow the mixture to cool.
4. Beat the egg whites until stiff and fold them gently into the mixture; pour this into a lightly buttered soufflé dish. Bake the soufflé in a preheated moderate oven (180°C/350°F, Gas Mark 4) for 25 to 30 minutes until the soufflé is set.

Celery au Gratin

METRIC/IMPERIAL	AMERICAN
2 heads celery	2 bunches celery
75 g/3 oz Gruyère or Cheddar cheese, grated	¾ cup grated Gruyère or Cheddar cheese
1 teaspoon Hungarian paprika	1 teaspoon Hungarian paprika

Also have ready: 300 ml/½ pint (1¼ cups) chicken stock

1. Use only the inner stalks at the heart of the celery, removing any tough strings. Cut the stalks into small chunks.
2. Bring the good chicken stock to the boil and add the celery, then simmer for 20 minutes, or until it is tender. Remove the celery with a slotted spoon and place in a shallow baking dish.
3. Pour some of the stock into the baking dish to a depth of about 1.25 cm/½ inch, then sprinkle the grated cheese evenly over the top. Season with a liberal sprinkling of paprika.
4. Place the dish under a hot grill (broiler) until the cheese melts and turns golden brown.

Couscous with Petits Pois

METRIC/IMPERIAL	AMERICAN
250 g/8 oz couscous	½ lb couscous
4 to 6 lettuce leaves, washed	4 to 6 lettuce leaves, washed
500 g/1 lb fresh or frozen petits pois	1 lb fresh or frozen petits pois

1. Couscous can be bought in most Eastern Mediterranean shops, packaged and par-cooked; prepare it according to the instructions on the packet. (It is simple to prepare in a steamer.)
2. Place the lettuce leaves in a pan over a medium heat and place the frozen or fresh peas on top – no other water is necessary. Cover the pan tightly and cook until tender; a few minutes for frozen peas, but up to 10 minutes for fresh. Add salt and a knob of butter and heat thoroughly.
3. Remove the lettuce leaves from the pan and shred them finely. Return the shreds to the pan with the couscous and mix into the peas.
4. Add more butter, salt and pepper to taste, and serve the couscous as an accompaniment to lamb or game.

Mangetout with Italian Ham

METRIC/IMPERIAL	AMERICAN
1 small onion	1 small onion
500 g/1 lb mangetout	3 cups snow peas
1 pinch sugar	1 pinch sugar
125 g/4 oz Italian or Spanish ham, diced	½ cup diced Italian or Spanish ham

Also have ready: 120 ml/4 fl oz (½ cup) chicken stock

1. Melt 4 tablespoons of butter in a saucepan with the whole onion, add the mangetout (snow peas), the sugar and chicken stock.
2. Cook quickly for about ten minutes, stirring.
3. Add the ham and reduce the heat. Cook until the mangetout are tender and all the liquid is absorbed (the onion can be removed at this stage if you wish).
4. If the ham is salty, further seasoning will not be necessary. Taste and add a pinch of salt if desired, then serve immediately.

Mangetout with Italian Ham: mangetout means 'eat-all', which is a clear indication of this dish's fate!

FINE ENDINGS

The arrival of the sweet at the table always causes a slight ripple of excitement. Even at the most sophisticated gathering there is usually a suppressed inclination to wonder 'What's for dessert?'

Whether you choose a tangy fruit dish or a light creamy concoction, the dessert should always be luscious and refreshing. It should be a delicious finale worth looking forward to, because, although they may not have finished their main course, you can rest assured that your guests will have left room for the sweet!

Summer Pudding

METRIC/IMPERIAL	AMERICAN
15 thin slices firm, white bread	15 thin slices firm, white bread
500 g/1 lb fresh raspberries, blackberries, redcurrants or blackcurrants (or a mixture)	1½ pints fresh raspberries, blackberries, red currants or black currants (or a mixture)
200 g/7 oz sugar (or to taste)	1 cup sugar (or to taste)
420 ml/¾ pint single cream	2 cups light cream

1. Cut the crusts from the bread and tile the inside and bottom of a large pudding basin (mold). Overlap the bread as you go around the sides, but do not overlap on the bottom. Save a few slices for the top of the pudding.
2. Purée and sieve (strain) the berries. (Currants and blackberries need to be briefly poached in water first.) Add sugar to taste and pour the fruit purée carefully into the bread-lined basin, saving a little to coat the finished pudding.
3. Cut the reserved slices of bread to fit as a lid. Place a small plate over this and weigh it down with cans of food. Place the bowl and weights in the refrigerator overnight.
4. To serve, carefully turn the summer pudding out onto a serving plate. Coat it with the reserved purée to give a fine pink colour, and serve with the cream.

Bavarian Blackcurrant Pudding

METRIC/IMPERIAL	AMERICAN
500 g/1 lb frozen blackcurrants, defrosted	1½ pints frozen black currants, thawed
125 g/4 oz sugar	½ cup sugar
250 ml/8 fl oz double cream	1 cup heavy cream
15 g/1 oz gelatine	1½ envelopes unflavored gelatin

1. Purée the blackcurrants in a blender, then press them through a fine sieve (strainer) to extract as much juice as possible. Discard the pulp.
2. Make a syrup by boiling the sugar in 125 ml/4 fl oz (½ cup) water for about 5 minutes. Remove the pan from the heat. Melt the gelatine in 3 tablespoons cold water over a low heat and add it to the syrup. Stir the syrup well and add the blackcurrant juice. Set the pan in cold water to cool the mixture down.
3. Whip two-thirds of the cream until it is foamy. Fold it gently into the blackcurrant mixture, pour into a lightly greased mould or individual moulds, and place in the refrigerator.
4. Leave the pudding in the refrigerator for several hours or, better still, make it 24 hours before you plan to eat it. Turn the pudding out onto a serving dish. Whip the rest of the cream with a teaspoon each of water and sugar to make chantilly cream, and use this to decorate the pudding.

Bavarian Blackcurrant Pudding:
a vivid little sweet loved by all ages and persuasions.

Bananas Flambé

METRIC/IMPERIAL	AMERICAN
4 firm bananas	*4 firm bananas*
4 tablespoons sugar	*¼ cup sugar*
1 teaspoon cinnamon (or to taste)	*1 teaspoon cinnamon (or to taste)*
120 ml/4 fl oz whisky	*½ cup Scotch whisky*

1. Melt 4 tablespoons butter in a heavy-bottomed frying pan (skillet) or in a chafing-dish at the table. Gently sauté the bananas and sprinkle them with the sugar and cinnamon.
2. When the bananas start to colour but are not too soft, heat all but 1 tablespoon of the whisky, ignite it, and pour it over the bananas.
3. Transfer the fruit to a warmed serving dish. Swish the juices around in the pan and pour them over the golden fruit.
4. Deglaze the pan by adding a little more butter and the remaining whisky, stir them over a medium heat to incorporate all the residues. Pour this over the bananas and serve.

Pear Fritters

METRIC/IMPERIAL	AMERICAN
8 pears, slightly underripe	*8 pears, slightly underripe*
150 g/5 oz mixed crystallized fruit, finely chopped	*1 cup finely chopped mixed candied fruit*
250 ml/8 fl oz lager	*1 cup light beer*
125 g/4 oz plain flour	*1 cup all-purpose flour*

1. Peel the pears. Core each one from the bottom to two-thirds up the pear, leaving the stem intact. Fill the core cavities with the crystallized fruit, packing it in tightly.
2. Mix the beer into the flour, a little at a time, to make a smooth batter. Coat the pears in the batter.
3. In a casserole that will hold the upright pears snugly, heat oil for deep frying. Test it with a drop of the batter; if it sizzles on contact, it is hot enough. Carefully lower in the pears so that they are standing in the oil, and cook them until they are golden brown. (The crystallized fruit will remain intact.)
4. Remove the pears with a large spoon or tongs and drain them briefly on paper towels before serving.

Poached Pears with Blackcurrant Jelly

METRIC/IMPERIAL	AMERICAN
4 firm pears	*4 firm pears*
350 g/12 oz blackcurrant or redcurrant jelly	*1 cup black currant or red currant jelly*
2 tablespoons cassis	*2 tablespoons cassis*
16 to 20 crystallized violets (optional)	*16 to 20 crystallized violets (optional)*

1. Peel the pears but leave their stems intact. Place them in a deep flameproof dish just large enough to hold them upright. Spoon the jelly in around them, then pour in enough water to cover the pears up to 2.5 cm/1 inch from the stems.
2. Cover the dish and bring the liquid to the boil. Lower the heat to a simmer and cook the pears for about 30 minutes (when you can stick a fork into them easily they are done). Remove the pears and set them aside to cool.
3. Boil the juice in the dish, uncovered, until reduced by about half. Cool, return the pears to the dish and pour over the cassis.
4. This dish improves with age, so let it stand overnight if you can. Before serving, decorate the pears around the stems with crystallized violets if desired.

Soused Watermelon

METRIC/IMPERIAL	AMERICAN
1 small watermelon	*1 small watermelon*
4 tablespoons Maraschino	*¼ cup Maraschino*
250 ml/8 fl oz dry white wine	*1 cup dry white wine*
2 tablespoons brandy	*2 tablespoons brandy*

1. Slice off the top of the watermelon and reserve it to make a lid.
2. Discard the seeds and scoop out the melon flesh. Shape it into small balls with a melonballer.
3. Pour the Maraschino, the wine and brandy onto the watermelon balls and allow to stand for at least 1 hour.
4. Put the watermelon and liquid in the watermelon 'pot' and replace the lid. Refrigerate for a couple of hours before serving.

Poached Pears with Blackcurrant Jelly: these blushing pears absorb the colour and flavour of the jelly to make a rare treat.

Chinese Glazed Apples

METRIC/IMPERIAL	AMERICAN
2 large green apples, cored, peeled and cut into 16 wedges each	2 large green apples, cored, peeled and cut into 16 wedges each
3 tablespoons flour, sifted	3 tablespoons flour, sifted
1 egg, whisked	1 egg, beaten
75 g/3 oz sugar	6 tablespoons sugar

1. Roll the apple slices in a little of the flour. Use the rest of the flour to make a batter with the egg, adding a tablespoon or so of water to make a smooth, thick consistency. Fold the apple slices through this batter.

2. In a pan, heat 1 tablespoon lard (shortening) with the sugar until the sugar has melted. Then add 2 tablespoons water, lower the heat and cook until the syrup colours.

3. In another pan, heat enough oil to deep-fry the apple wedges a few at a time; cook each batch for about 2 minutes. As they are cooked, drain the apple pieces and coat them with the syrup. Have ready a bowl of iced water.

4. Transfer the syrup-coated apples to a warm, lightly greased bowl. Take it to the table with the bowl of iced water, where the guests will pull the apple pieces apart with chopsticks. The apple slices with their streaming sugar threads are plunged into the iced water; the sugar sets into a hard glaze but the apple inside remains satisfyingly hot.

Tarte Tatin: every French restaurant claims its Tatin is the best in the world. Here's one version of this classic.

Apples Bonne Femme

METRIC/IMPERIAL	AMERICAN
4 apples	4 apples
4 slices white bread	4 slices white bread
4 tablespoons sugar	4 tablespoons sugar
150 ml/¼ pint cream	⅔ cup light cream

1. Core the apples and peel a third of the skin from their tops.

2. Toast the bread, butter it liberally, and sprinkle it with a little of the sugar.

3. Lay the pieces of toast side by side in a buttered baking dish. Put each apple on a piece of toast, and fill the centres with sugar. Place a pat of butter on top of each apple.

4. Bake the apples in a preheated moderate oven (180°C/350°F, Gas Mark 4) for about 30 minutes, basting occasionally with the juices in the dish, until they are soft but not mushy. Serve the apples with the cream.

Tarte Tatin

METRIC/IMPERIAL	AMERICAN
75 g/3 oz sugar	⅓ cup sugar
2 teaspoons wine vinegar	2 teaspoons wine vinegar
1 kg/2 lb cooking apples	2 lb tart apples
250 g/8 oz frozen shortcrust pastry	½ lb frozen basic pie dough

1. You will need a 23 cm/9 inch metal flat tin (pie pan), 4 cm/1½ inches deep. Place the tin over a medium heat and melt the sugar and vinegar with 50 g/2 oz (¼ cup) butter. Stir gently until the mixture is a golden toffee colour. Set aside (do not worry if it congeals, it will melt during cooking later).

2. Peel, core and slice the apples. Arrange them over the caramel mixture in a wheel shape, making sure the surface is level.

3. Dot the top with butter and sprinkle with a little more sugar. Roll out the pastry (pie dough) and cut to fit the inside of the tin. Carefully lay it over the apples. Bake the tart in a preheated moderately hot oven (200°C/400°F, Gas Mark 6) for 35 to 40 minutes. If the pastry begins to colour too fast, cover it with a sheet of foil for the rest of the cooking time.

4. Remove from the oven and run a knife around between the side of the tart and the tin. Turn smartly out onto a warm serving dish so that the pastry is underneath and the apples and caramel on top. Serve warm or cold with cream if desired.

Omelette Soufflé Flambé

METRIC/IMPERIAL	AMERICAN
6 eggs, separated, plus 2 egg whites	6 eggs, separated, plus 2 egg whites
125 g/4 oz sugar	½ cup sugar
1 teaspoon vanilla essence	1 teaspoon vanilla
1 to 2 tablespoons Grand Marnier	1 to 2 tablespoons Grand Marnier

1.   Beat the six egg yolks with the sugar and vanilla essence until light and smooth.
2.   Beat the eight egg whites until they are very stiff, then fold into them the yolks and sugar mixture. The mixture should be very light.
3.   Sprinkle a large buttered baking dish with a little more sugar, and pour the soufflé mixture into it. Bake the soufflé in a preheated moderately hot oven (200°C/400°F, Gas Mark 6) for about 10 to 12 minutes until it is risen and golden.
4.   Warm the Grand Marnier in a ladle at the table. Pour it over the soufflé, ignite it and serve immediately.

Apricot Soufflé

METRIC/IMPERIAL	AMERICAN
½ lb dried apricots	1¼ cups dried apricots
4 egg whites	4 egg whites
1 scant tablespoon sugar	1 scant tablespoon sugar
2 oz ground toasted almonds	½ cup ground toasted almonds

1.   Place the apricots in a saucepan and add enough water just to cover them. Simmer the apricots for about 35 minutes until they are soft. Leave them to cool a little, then purée them in a blender. Pass the purée through a sieve (strainer) into a bowl and discard any fibrous residue left in the sieve.
2.   In another bowl, beat the egg whites stiffly. Gently fold them into the apricots.
3.   Butter a soufflé dish and sprinkle with the sugar. Spoon the apricot mixture into the dish and place it in a preheated moderate oven (180°C/350°F, Gas Mark 4) for 15 to 20 minutes.
4.   Scatter the toasted almonds over the top of the soufflé and serve immediately.

Marmalade Omelette Soufflé

METRIC/IMPERIAL	AMERICAN
6 eggs, separated	6 eggs, separated
2 tablespoons Seville marmalade	2 tablespoons Seville marmalade
1 tablespoon icing sugar	1 tablespoon confectioners' sugar
1 tablespoon grated orange rind	1 tablespoon grated orange rind

1.   Beat the egg yolks with 5 tablespoons water until frothy. Beat the whites stiffly and fold them into the yolks.
2.   Melt 2 tablespoons clarified butter in a frying pan (skillet), making sure that it coats the sides as well as the bottom of the pan. Pour in the omelette mixture and cook it over a low flame until it becomes lightly coloured and puffy.
3.   Gently warm the marmalade in a small saucepan and spread it over the omelette. Carefully fold one half of the omelette over onto the other half.
4.   Dust the top of the omelette with a mixture of icing (confectioners') sugar and orange rind, and score it with a hot salamander or skewer.

Marmalade Omelette Soufflé: although this can be whipped up quickly for an unexpected guest, it looks and tastes superb.

Frozen Soufflé with Grand Marnier

METRIC/IMPERIAL	AMERICAN
125 g/4 oz sugar	½ cup sugar
3 eggs, separated, plus 2 yolks	3 eggs, separated, plus 2 yolks
6 tablespoons Grand Marnier	6 tablespoons Grand Marnier
300 ml/½ pint double cream	1¼ cups heavy cream

1. Boil the sugar with 2 to 3 tablespoons water until it drips off the spoon in a thin, thread-like trickle.
2. Pour this syrup into the egg yolks and beat until the mixture thickens and foams; set aside to cool. Stir in the Grand Marnier.
3. Whip the cream lightly and fold it into the mixture. Whip the egg whites stiffly and fold them into the mixture.
4. Spoon the mixture into the soufflé dish and freeze it for several hours before serving.

Cold Chocolate Soufflé

METRIC/IMPERIAL	AMERICAN
300 g/10 oz plain chocolate	10 squares semi-sweet chocolate
2 tablespoons brandy	2 tablespoons brandy
1 to 2 tablespoons instant coffee	1 to 2 tablespoons instant coffee
8 eggs, separated	8 eggs, separated

1. Melt the chocolate with the brandy and coffee over a low heat. Beat the egg yolks.
2. When the chocolate has melted, stir it into the egg yolks, incorporating it well. Leave the mixture to cool.
3. Beat the egg whites and fold them into the cooled yolk and chocolate mixture; pour into a serving dish or individual dishes.
4. Allow the mousse to stand in a cool place (not the refrigerator) for about 4 hours before serving Decorate with a little whipped cream and extra chocolate if desired.

Cold Chocolate Soufflé: even soufflé experts are impressed by this creation. And it's so easy!

Chocolate Orange Mousse

METRIC/IMPERIAL	AMERICAN
75 g/3 oz plain chocolate	3 squares (3 oz) semi-sweet chocolate
1 small orange	1 small orange
50 g/2 oz caster sugar	¼ cup superfine sugar
3 eggs, separated	3 eggs, separated

1. Melt the chocolate in the top of a double boiler over simmering water. Add 65 g/2½ oz (⅓ cup) butter and beat together well with a whisk.
2. Finely grate the orange rind and squeeze its juice; add both to the chocolate, with the sugar. Beat the ingredients together well. Carefully add the egg yolks, one at a time, blending all the while.
3. Beat the egg whites until they are stiff and fold them into the mixture, then transfer it to a serving bowl.
4. Chill the mousse until set. If desired, decorate with grated chocolate before serving.

Blackberry and Maple Syrup Mousse

METRIC/IMPERIAL	AMERICAN
4 egg yolks	4 egg yolks
150 g/5 oz maple syrup, warmed	½ cup maple syrup, warmed
300 ml/½ pint double cream	1¼ cups heavy cream
350 g/12 oz fresh or frozen blackberries	1 pint fresh or frozen blackberries

1. In a large heatproof bowl, beat the egg yolks until they are thick and creamy. Gradually beat in the warm maple syrup. Stand the bowl in a pan of simmering water over a low heat and cook until slightly thickened, beating all the while. Remove the bowl from the pan and leave the mixture to cool.
2. In a separate bowl, whip the cream until it forms peaks, and fold it into the egg and maple syrup mixture.
3. Purée the blackberries in a blender and press through a strainer to remove the seeds. Carefully fold two-thirds of the purée into the mixture. Spoon this into a mould and freeze overnight.
4. Turn the mousse out, and decorate with the remaining blackberry purée. Allow to stand for a few minutes before serving.

Orange Flummery

METRIC/IMPERIAL	AMERICAN
75 g/3 oz sugar	1/3 cup sugar
3 eggs, separated	3 eggs, separated
juice and grated zest of 2 oranges	juice and grated zest of 2 oranges
juice of 1 small lemon	juice of 1 small lemon

1. Bring the sugar and 6 tablespoons water to the boil in a saucepan. Simmer for approximately 10 minutes, stirring constantly, until you have a syrup that will coat the back of the spoon.
2. Beat the egg yolks until they are fluffy, then continue to beat while slowly pouring in the hot syrup (this is easier with an electric beater). Blend the citrus juice and zest into the mixture.
3. Beat the egg whites until they are stiff and fold them into the yolk and syrup mixture.
4. Pour the flummery into a soufflé dish or bowl; chill it for 1 hour before serving.

Chilled Lemon Dessert

METRIC/IMPERIAL	AMERICAN
4 eggs, separated	4 eggs, separated
5 tablespoons caster sugar	5 tablespoons sugar
juice and grated rind of 2 lemons	juice and grated rind of 2 lemons
2 teaspoons gelatine	2 teaspoons unflavored gelatin

1. Beat the egg yolks with the sugar, lemon juice and zest in a double boiler over boiling water.
2. When the mixture thickens, remove the pan and cool rapidly by placing it over a bed of ice cubes until it is quite cold. Beat well.
3. Melt the gelatine in 4 tablespoons of cold water over a low heat. Cool and add it to the cold mixture, beating hard all the time.
4. Whip the egg whites with a pinch of salt. Mix a heaped tablespoon of egg white into the mixture, then fold the rest in carefully. Chill for approximately 4 hours before serving.

Passion Fruit Fool

METRIC/IMPERIAL	AMERICAN
8 passion fruit	8 passion fruit
2 to 3 tablespoons sugar	2 to 3 tablespoons sugar
200 ml/1/3 pint double cream	7/8 cup heavy cream
25 g/1 oz shelled pistachio nuts	2 tablespoons shelled pistachio nuts

1. Cut the tops off the passion fruit. Carefully spoon out the flesh. Pass through a sieve (strainer) to remove the seeds if you do not like their texture. Add the sugar to the puréed fruit.
2. Whip the cream until stiff and fold the fruit into it.
3. Divide the fool between four wine glasses and chill for at least 2 hours.
4. Blanch the pistachio nuts briefly in boiling water and peel off all the brown skin. Whizz them in a blender for 30 seconds, and sprinkle them over the fool before serving.

Passion Fruit Fool: a dessert which is guaranteed to bring romance into your life!

Zabaglione

METRIC/IMPERIAL
4 egg yolks
4 tablespoons Marsala, sherry or cognac
2 tablespoons icing sugar
8 langues de chat

AMERICAN
4 egg yolks
¼ cup Marsala wine, sherry or cognac
2 tablespoons confectioners' sugar
8 langues de chat

1. Whip the egg yolks in a bowl with the wine and sugar.
2. Pour the yolk mixture into the top part of a double boiler, placed over gently simmering water.
3. Whisk the mixture gently for about 15 minutes.
4. The mixture is done when it becomes thick and foamy and sticks to the whisk. Spoon it into individual serving dishes or wine glasses and accompany with the *langues de chat*.

Crème Brulée

METRIC/IMPERIAL
600 ml / 1 pint single cream
4 egg yolks, thoroughly beaten
2 tablespoons rum or Amaretto
5 to 6 tablespoons brown sugar

AMERICAN
2½ cups light cream
4 egg yolks, thoroughly beaten
2 tablespoons rum or Amaretto
5 to 6 tablespoons brown sugar

1. Bring the cream to the boil and keep it on a low boil, stirring constantly, for 1 minute. Remove it from the heat and continue to beat while slowly pouring in the egg yolks.
2. Transfer the mixture to the top of a double boiler and cook for 5 more minutes until it thickens. Stir in the rum or Amaretto.
3. Divide the cream between four ramekins. Let the cream cool and then chill in the refrigerator.
4. Just before serving, cover the surface of the cream with a thin layer of brown sugar, and place the ramekins under the grill (broiler) for a few minutes until the sugar has caramelized.

Oranges in Zabaglione Sauce

METRIC/IMPERIAL
4 oranges
5 tablespoons sugar
3 egg yolks
1 tablespoon Curaçao or Cointreau

AMERICAN
4 oranges
5 tablespoons sugar
3 egg yolks
1 tablespoon Curaçao or Cointreau

1. Pare the rind of 1 orange and cut it into tiny strips. Peel the oranges, divide them into sections and skin each section over a bowl to catch the juice.
2. Steep the juice, orange sections and rind together with 2 tablespoons sugar for about 30 minutes. Drain off the juice and set it aside. Divide the pieces of orange and strips of rind between four individual ovenproof dishes.
3. Put the egg yolks, the sweetened juice, the liqueur and 2 tablespoons sugar into a large heatproof bowl and beat them together. Place the bowl in a pan of simmering water and continue to beat for 7 to 8 minutes, until the egg yolks are foamy and thick. Spoon the mixture over the orange sections and sprinkle each portion with a little of the remaining sugar.
4. Place the custard dishes briefly under a hot grill (broiler) to melt the sugar and form a thin golden crust; take care not to let them burn. Serve immediately.

Oranges in Zabaglione Sauce: Zabaglione has a reputation for being more difficult to make than it really is; don't be put off.

Mock Fontainebleau à la Crème

METRIC/IMPERIAL
*500 ml / 18 fl oz full-fat
natural yogurt
1 litre / 1¾ pints single cream
sugar to taste
fresh raspberries to decorate
(optional)*

AMERICAN
*2¼ cups full-fat natural
yogurt
4¼ cups light cream
sugar to taste
fresh raspberries to decorate
(optional)*

1. Cover a big sieve (strainer) with a layer of cheesecloth. Pour the yogurt into the cloth and add a pinch of salt. Place the sieve over a bowl; the whey will drip into it, leaving a firm curd in the sieve. This process will take 4 to 5 hours.
2. In the meantime, when a little whey has collected in the bowl, take 2 teaspoons of it and stir it into the cream. Let it stand for about 30 minutes, after which time it will be a reasonable approximation of true French *crème fraiche*. (Another possible substitute is a combination of half cream and half soured cream. Neither of these is quite the same as crème fraiche, however.)
3. Remove the curd from the cheesecloth and spoon it into individual dishes. The curd is so concentrated that, though it may seem small, one rounded tablespoon per serving is probably enough. Pour two or three tablespoons of the treated cream over each tablespoon of the curd.
4. To serve, sprinkle each portion with sugar to taste, and decorate with raspberries.

Crème Caramel

METRIC/IMPERIAL
*250 g / 8 oz sugar
2 eggs, plus 3 yolks
5 tablespoons single cream
350 ml / 12 fl oz milk, heated
with a vanilla pod*

AMERICAN
*1 cup sugar
2 eggs, plus 3 yolks
⅓ cup light cream
1½ cups milk, heated with a
vanilla bean*

1. Heat two-thirds of the sugar with 5 tablespoons of water for 3 to 4 minutes over moderate heat or until the syrup is a light caramel colour. Remove from the heat and pour the syrup into four individual, ovenproof moulds. Swish the syrup around so that it completely covers the bottoms. Set them aside.
2. Beat the eggs and yolks with the cream and the rest of the sugar until very smooth.
3. Blend the hot milk into this mixture with a whisk. Pour this into the moulds.
4. Place the moulds in a pan of hot water in a preheated moderate oven (160°C/325°F, Gas Mark 3) for 45 minutes. Test with a fork to see if they are set. Allow to cool and slide a knife around the edge of each mould. Turn the crèmes out onto serving plates.

Syllabub

METRIC/IMPERIAL
*1 lemon
300 ml / ½ pint double cream
125 g / 4 oz caster sugar
300 ml / ½ pint sherry*

AMERICAN
*1 lemon
1¼ cups heavy cream
½ cup superfine sugar
1¼ cups sherry*

1. Finely grate the lemon rind, taking care only to remove the zest.
2. Halve and squeeze the lemon and strain the juice.
3. Put the cream, sugar and sherry in a bowl and add the lemon rind and juice.
4. Whisk all the ingredients together well, and pour the syllabub into little pots. Refrigerate the syllabub for about 2 hours before serving.

*Mock Fontainebleau à la Crème: a very good
imitation of the real Fontainebleau and just as delicious.*

Roman Ricotta Dessert

METRIC/IMPERIAL	AMERICAN
250 g/8 oz Ricotta cheese, or any curd cheese	*1 cup Ricotta cheese, or any curd cheese*
2 tablespoons icing sugar	*2 tablespoons confectioners' sugar*
3 tablespoons finely ground instant coffee or cocoa powder	*2 tablespoons finely ground instant coffee or unsweetened cocoa*
4 tablespoons brandy	*¼ cup brandy*

1. Put the cheese into a bowl and add the sugar and coffee. Blend them together well with a fork.
2. Add the brandy to the bowl and stir in until the mixture is smooth.
3. Taste the mixture and add more coffee, brandy or sugar as desired.
4. Transfer the dessert to a serving bowl or individual dishes. Sift a thin layer of powdered coffee on top, and refrigerate the dessert for 2 hours, or until firm.

Petits Pots au Chocolat

METRIC/IMPERIAL	AMERICAN
200 g/7 oz plain chocolate	*7 squares semi-sweet chocolate*
300 ml/½ pint double cream	*1¼ cups heavy cream*
2 to 3 drops vanilla essence	*2 to 3 drops vanilla*
1 egg, lightly beaten	*1 egg, lightly beaten*

1. Break up the chocolate into fairly small pieces and melt it in the top of a double boiler over simmering water. Heat the cream in another saucepan and, as it begins to boil, pour it onto the chocolate. Stir them together until smooth.
2. Add the vanilla to the chocolate with a tiny pinch of salt and the egg.
3. Stir the mixture until it is creamy.
4. Pour the creamy chocolate into small individual pots. Chill the 'petits pots' for several hours before serving.

Ile Flotant

METRIC/IMPERIAL	AMERICAN
4 eggs, separated	*4 eggs, separated*
65 g/2½ oz sugar	*⅓ cup sugar*
500 ml/18 fl oz milk	*2¼ cups milk*
1½ teaspoons vanilla essence	*1½ teaspoons vanilla*

1. Beat the egg yolks lightly while adding 3 tablespoons of the sugar and a pinch of salt.
2. Heat the milk in the top of a double boiler over simmering water, but do not allow it to boil. While stirring gently, add the egg yolks to the milk and cook until the mixture begins to thicken.
3. Pour the mixture into a baking dish, stir in 1 teaspoon vanilla and set aside to cool.
4. To make the meringues, beat the egg whites until they are stiff, gradually adding the rest of the sugar and ½ teaspoon vanilla. Shape small mounds of the meringue mixture with a spoon and drop them onto the cooled custard. Bake the dish in a preheated very hot oven (240°C/475°F, Gas Mark 9) for 2 to 3 minutes, or until the meringue begins to colour slightly and becomes crisp. This dish is good either hot or cold.

Roman Ricotta Dessert: any curd cheese will suffice in this recipe, but only Ricotta gives the true Italian taste.

Tea and Lime Sorbet

METRIC/IMPERIAL	AMERICAN
250 g/8 oz sugar	1 cup sugar
3 fresh limes	3 fresh limes
8 to 10 teaspoons tea or good tea bags	8 to 10 teaspoons tea or good tea bags

1. Make a syrup by dissolving the sugar in 900 ml/1½ pints (3¾ cups) water over a low heat. Boil the syrup for 2 to 3 minutes until it is clear.
2. Finely peel the limes and simmer the rinds in a third of the syrup, stirring constantly, for about 10 minutes. (Do not allow the syrup to burn.) Strain the syrup and reserve. Discard the rinds.
3. In a separate pan, bring the remaining syrup to the boil and add the tea. Remove the syrup from the heat and allow the tea to steep in it for 5 minutes only; strain the tea leaves or remove the tea bags. Squeeze the limes and strain the juice into the tea-flavoured syrup.
4. Combine the two syrups and blend them well. Taste the mixture and add more sugar or lime juice if desired. Pour the sorbet (sherbet) into a container and place in the freezer for 2 to 3 hours, stirring occasionally to prevent it from crystallizing. Freeze the sorbet.

Baked Pineapple Alaska

METRIC/IMPERIAL	AMERICAN
1 very ripe pineapple	1 very ripe pineapple
600 ml/1 pint vanilla ice cream	2½ cups vanilla ice cream
2 tablespoons desiccated coconut	2 tablespoons shredded coconut
4 egg whites	4 egg whites

1. Slice the pineapple in half lengthwise. Remove the core and scoop out the flesh; chop it or whizz it briefly in a blender or food processor. Discard the hard core if you wish, although it is perfectly edible. Drain off the juice from the pulp, it makes a nice drink.
2. Mix the pineapple pulp with the ice cream and pack the mixture into the halves of the pineapple shell. Sprinkle the coconut over the top and place in the freezer, until very hard.
4. Just before serving, beat the egg whites stiffly and spread over the pineapple halves. Put them into a preheated hot oven (230°C/450°F, Gas Mark 8) for 3 minutes, or until the egg whites colour. Allow to stand for a few minutes before serving. It's spectacular!

Lee's Fig and Pernod Ice Cream

METRIC/IMPERIAL	AMERICAN
1 × 875 g/1 lb 12 oz can green figs in syrup	1 × 1 lb 12 oz can green figs in syrup
juice of 1 lemon	juice of 1 lemon
3 tablespoons Pernod	3 tablespoons Pernod
250 ml/8 fl oz double cream	1 cup heavy cream

1. Purée the figs and syrup in a blender, then press them through a sieve (strainer) into a mixing bowl. (You can add a tablespoonful of the seeds to the purée if you like the texture.)
2. Add the lemon juice, a pinch of salt and the Pernod to the purée and stir well.
3. Whip the cream and fold it evenly into the fig mixture, then pour into a container.
4. Put the mixture into the freezer for 2 to 3 hours, stirring occasionally to prevent it crystallizing.

Lee's Fig and Pernod Ice Cream: a creamy dessert with an indescribably smooth and subtle flavour

90

Strawberry-Raspberry Ice Cream

METRIC/IMPERIAL
1 × 375 g / 13 oz can
strawberries
1 × 375 g / 13 oz can
raspberries
600 ml / 1 pint single cream

AMERICAN
1 × 13 oz can strawberries
1 × 13 oz can raspberries
2½ cups light cream

1. Drain the fruit, reserving about one-third of the juice.
2. Lightly whip the cream until it is fluffy but not stiff.
3. Fold the fruit and the reserved juice into the cream and transfer the mixture to a container.
4. Freeze the mixture for 2 to 3 hours, stirring occasionally to prevent the ice cream from crystallizing.

Mango Ice

METRIC/IMPERIAL
125 g / 4 oz sugar
2 ripe mangoes
juice of 1 lemon

AMERICAN
½ cup sugar
2 ripe mangoes
juice of 1 lemon

1. Make a syrup with the sugar and 120 ml / 4 fl oz (½ cup) water. Boil it for 3 to 4 minutes until it is lightly coloured and falls off the spoon in a thin trickle.
2. Peel the mangoes and slice the flesh. Set aside four slivers for decoration and mash the rest with a fork.
3. Add the lemon juice to the sugar syrup and mix it thoroughly. Add the mangoes to this, and beat in well.
4. Pour the mixture into an ice tray and freeze for 2 to 3 hours, stirring from time to time to prevent ice crystals from forming. Decorate the water ice with the slivers of mango and serve.

Caffè Granita

METRIC/IMPERIAL
125 g / 4 oz sugar
500 ml / 18 fl oz very strong
espresso coffee or strong
instant coffee made with 4
teaspoons coffee powder
120 ml / 4 fl oz Crème de Cacao

AMERICAN
½ cup sugar
2¼ cups very strong espresso
coffee or strong instant
coffee made with 4
teaspoons coffee powder
½ cup Crème de Cacao

1. Bring 250 ml / 8 fl oz (1 cup) water to the boil and pour in the sugar. Let the mixture boil for 3 minutes but do not stir. Add this to the coffee, and set aside to cool.
2. When cool, pour the mixture into an ice tray and put in the freezer for several hours, stirring occasionally, until it is frozen. It will look crystalline.
3. Scrape the coffee ice with a spoon until it resembles rough snow.
4. Divide the ice between 4 individual dishes and spoon a little Crème de Cacao over each portion. Serve with whipped cream if desired.

Caffè Granita:
a refreshing Italian ice with a cool and crunchy texture.

INDEX

—— PUBLISHER'S ACKNOWLEDGEMENTS ——

Photography: Martin Brigdale
Photographic styling: Sue Russell
Preparation of food for photography: Liz and Pete
Photographer's assistansts: Nick Carman and Steve Hyde

The Publisher would also like to thank the following for the loan of props for photography: *page 6* glass jug, salt and pepper mills, and *page 8* oyster knife from David Mellor, 4 Sloane Square, London SW1; *page 12* knife by Boda Nova, and plates 'Trio' by Villeroy and Boch from Heals, Tottenham Court Road, London WC1; *page 15* plates by Celadon from Heals; *page 28* gratin dish by Le Creuset only from Elizabeth David, 46 Bourne Street, London SW1; *page 35* platter by Arzberg from major stockists; *page 43* plate 'Silver Line' by Burleigh from Heals; *page 44* platter 'Angelo Gris' from Heals; *page 47* platter from The Conran Shop, 77 Fulham Road, London SW3; *page 82* glass and jug from The Glass House, 65 Long Acre, London WC2.

—— AUTHOR'S ACKNOWLEDGEMENTS ——

This book has been a joint effort – including much testing and tasting – on the part of a number of people, particularly my wife, Bettina, and my daughter, Claudia, without whose perseverance it would never have materialized.

I would also like to thank those friends and colleagues who have had the kindness to allow me to use variations on, or adaptations of, their recipes:

the late James Beard for Poulet à la Basquaise, and Omelette Soufflée Flambée from *Paris Cuisine* (Little, Brown and Co.); Giuseppe Bellini for his Watermelon Surprise; Betty Carlin for her Caviar Pie; Craig Claiborne for his Flourless Cheese Soufflé; the Committee Interprofessionel du Vin de Champagne for Oysters in Champagne Sauce; Elizabeth David for her Apricot Soufflé, Poireaux à la Provençale, and Les Perdreaux aux Raisins from *Mediterranean Food* (Penguin Books), and for Spaghetti con Salsa di Zucchine from *Italian Food* (Penguin Books); Francis and Jenny Guth for Broadbean Tortilla, and Tuna and Lettuce Omelette; Nancy and Arthur Hawkins for Roast Loin of Pork with Cranberry Glaze, and Portuguese Pork with Clams from *Nantucket and Other New England Cooking* (Hasting House Publishers); Elisabeth Lambert Ortiz for Rouget Grillé au Fenouil, and Sole au Vermouth from her book *Cooking with the Young Chefs of France* (M. Evans and Co. Inc.); Bépy Tome for Tagliolini with Whisky and Smoked Salmon, and Pasta Shells with Green Tuna Sauce; Roger Vergé of the Restaurant Moulins de Mougins, for his Fish with Orange and Lemon, and his Oranges in Sabayon; Anne Willan of L'École de Cuisine la Varenne, for her Tea and Lime Sorbet.

My thanks, too, to Marita Byrne, Isabel Papadakis and Carole Thomas of Octopus Books, who took time and trouble over the production of this book.

Henry McNulty